ECHOING THE WORD:
The Ministry of Forming Disciples

Grant S. Sperry-White

DISCIPLESHIP RESOURCES

P.O. BOX 840 • NASHVILLE, TENNESSEE 37202-0840

www.discipleshipresources.org

Library of Congress Card Catalog No. 96-86592

ISBN 0-88177-177-5

DR177

CONTENTS

ABBREVIATIONS

AJ   *Accompanying the Journey: A Handbook for Sponsors* (1997) by Lester Ruth

BWS   *By Water and the Spirit: Making Connections for Identity and Ministry* (1997) by Gayle Carlton Felton

COCU   Consultation on Church Union

CTW   *Come to the Waters: Baptism & Our Ministry of Welcoming Seekers & Making Disciples* (1996) by Daniel Benedict Jr.

GV   *Gracious Voices: Shouts & Whispers for God Seekers* (1997) by William P. McDonald

MV   *Mil Voces Para Celebrar: Himnario Metodista* (1996) Spanish-language United Methodist Hymnal

UMBOW   *The United Methodist Book of Worship* (1992)

UMH   *The United Methodist Hymnal* (1989)

WCC   World Council of Churches

PREFACE

If you are reading this resource, chances are that your pastor or another person has asked you to serve as a catechist. If so, this book's content is designed to help you discern God's call through this ministry.

Echoing the Word will describe what a catechist does. It will show how this ministry fits into the overall pattern of Christian initiation presented in *Come to the Waters: Baptism & Our Ministry of Welcoming Seekers & Making Disciples* and its companion volumes, *By Water and the Spirit: Making Connections for Identity and Ministry, Accompanying the Journey: A Handbook for Sponsors,* and *Gracious Voices: Shouts & Whispers for God Seekers.* (Since I frequently refer to *Come to the Waters* in this book, I suggest that you have a copy easily available as you read *Echoing the Word.*)

As a catechist, you will play a major role in the formation of new Christians. The premise of this book is that a catechist labors to foster, nurture, and develop the Christian faith and practices of a particular group: people who have decided to begin the journey of becoming a Christian through formation (the time leading up to baptism) and through integration into the life of the church after baptism. *Echoing the Word* provides the basic tools with which to fulfill this ministry in concert with the pastor, the sponsors, and the congregation.

Your ministry as catechist is diverse; yet, it involves some well-defined areas. The chapters of this book focus on these areas. The first chapter introduces you to the process of Christian initiation, the ministry of a catechist, and the concept of formation. Chapters Two through Five discuss the main ingredients of your ministry: Scripture, worship, prayer and the disciplined life, and ministry in daily life. Each chapter suggests ways to relate the subject to the four stages of the initiation journey: inquiry, formation, intensive preparation, and integration. You will learn how to connect each topic to the specific steps people take toward baptism and beyond.

The chapters are geared to the initiation of adults who have never been baptized. However, Chapter Six discusses how you can adapt the formation process for returning members and for infants and children. There is a list of resources at the end of each chapter. The book concludes with two appendices: a sample outline for a formational group session and an order of service for commissioning a catechist.

In *Echoing the Word* I occasionally liken the work of a catechist to that of a gardener. A gardener labors to nurture the plants in her garden, using her knowledge to foster their growth and development through a variety of means: fertilizing, weeding, planting, working the earth, searching diligently for signs of growth and for the first signs of pests or disease. She knows that each plant is different and has its own requirements: sun or shade, sandy or rich soil. Yet, the seeds and plants mysteriously grow on their own. The gardener does her work, having faith in the unseen process that produces a plant from seed to fruit. Of course, a gardener also knows that the success of a garden depends on other factors out of her control: sun, rain, the temperature, insects. The point is that your ministry as a catechist—as a "gardener"—is very important for the formation of new Christians, and yet ultimately the mystery of coming to faith and being formed in Christian identity is God's, and God's alone.

So you do not need to feel daunted as you approach this work or to feel pressured to guarantee that large numbers of people decide to be baptized. The work of salvation is God's, and the leaven of the reign of God works slowly and in ways we often cannot see. As the parable of the sower makes clear, God sows the seed of the Word lavishly and generously, but not all seeds will grow to bear fruit. (See Matthew 13:3-9, 18-23; Mark 4:3-9, 13-20; Luke 8:5-8, 11-15.) The most we can do as faithful servants is watch for the sprouting of the Word in human hearts and do all we can to cooperate with God's grace as it mysteriously works to bring about faith that bears fruit.

This is a particularly exciting time to be involved in Christian formation in The United Methodist Church. Because United Methodists had not embarked on an experiment in Christian initiation like the one proposed in *Come to the Waters*, I have felt as if I were in uncharted territory during the writing of this book. The United Methodist Church is a diverse communion in which a number of traditions—racial and ethnic as well as theological—live together in a creative tension. Far from trying to impose a rigid structure of baptismal formation on such a diverse church, I propose *one* way of being the church today, and that is the way illustrated in *Come to the Waters*. Most of all, I want to stimulate your creativity as you give your time and gifts to the ministry of forming Christians who will become the faithful disciples the world needs.

I write these pages as an historian of Christianity and Christian liturgy, not as a theologian or a specialist in Christian religious education. Therefore, I have had to rely on the expertise and wisdom of many people. The setting for many of the ideas in this book was a course entitled "Didache: Church as Community of Christian Formation," which I team-taught with my colleague Dr. Sondra Matthaei during the fall 1996 semester at Saint Paul School of Theology. I am grateful to the members of this class whose questions, comments, and insights have helped greatly in shaping my thoughts about Christian formation. I owe a particular word of thanks to Dr. Matthaei. Her ideas, enthusiasm for the ministry of formation in the church, knowledge of Wesleyan tradition, and encouragement have been invaluable. I also wish to thank the people of Broadway Christian Parish United Methodist Church in South Bend, Indiana, their former pastor, Sara Webb Phillips, and their present pastor, Michael Mather. This faithful community was our church home for a number of years. Its positive and loving influences helped form my vision of the church as a body empowered for loving ministry in the world. The members of this congregation have shared their wisdom. I dedicate this book to them. During and after our time in South Bend, Mike Mather has given me the gift of stimulating and provocative conversation about ministry today.

I am grateful to the Rev. Daniel T. Benedict Jr., who invited me to write this resource and whose prayers and encouragement have supported me during the writing process. Last but not least, I owe a great debt of thanks to my wife Beth, without whose encouragement, sense of humor, and steadfast support this book would not have been possible.

Grant S. Sperry-White

Chapter One

THE CATECHIST, FORMATION, AND CHRISTIAN INITIATION

O taste and see that the LORD is good....
(Psalm 34:8)

Happy are those who live in your house,
ever singing your praise.
(Psalm 84:4)

This chapter lays the foundation for the rest of the book. It raises a number of issues about the catechist, about formation, and about Christian initiation. Three of these issues are at the heart of your ministry as catechist:
- What does "formation" mean?
- Who is the catechist?
- What does the catechist do?

By the end of the chapter, you should have a clear idea of what this ministry is all about and how it fits in the process of initiation as a whole.

WHAT DOES CHRISTIAN FORMATION MEAN?

The sub-title of this book—*The Ministry of Forming Disciples*—provides a clue to the heart of your work as catechist: to *form, shape,* and *nurture* people for the daily, life-long, joyous, and arduous pilgrimage of Christian discipleship.

The task of Christian formation *(catechesis)* is without a doubt one of the most important in the church today. If we in the church do not integrate newcomers in a new way of living daily life, if we do not provide initiates and the newly-baptized with the life-giving Word for all areas of their lives, we may have succeeded in the short-term goal of bringing people to Christ; but we will have failed in our aim of making lifelong disciples.

In the late twentieth century, many churches—including The United Methodist Church—have begun to realize what early Christians in the first centuries already knew: The life of discipleship is one of ongoing formation. Indeed, this makes your ministry of forming disciples very exciting. Your work is part of a new venture in the church today, but it has deep roots in the life of the Christian church through the centuries.

WHAT FORMATION IS NOT AND WHAT FORMATION IS

To help you understand what "forming disciples" is all about, let's begin by saying what formation is *not*. Formation is not simply

- teaching people correct doctrine, although church teaching is a part of the process.
- becoming familiar and comfortable with the church's liturgical celebrations, although the experience of worship is an important part of the journey.
- learning another way of being good to people, although the love of God and love of one's neighbor are the core of Christian life.
- another type of church school class or confirmation class.

Christian formation *is* the process of making disciples in heart, in mind, and in body. It involves the church asking a hard question of the people seeking to become United Methodist Christians: Will you enter into a lengthy, intensive process of Christian initiation in which you will learn a new way of life that leads to baptism, to the laying on of hands, and to Holy Communion and in which you are adopted by God into a new family? It is in the family of the church that people come to learn what it means to be a disciple of Jesus Christ every day of their lives. Nothing less will suffice if we as the church intend to be faithful to God's call to make disciples.

THE CONTEXT OF FORMATION

Implied in the previous paragraph is the basic concept that undergirds this book, as well as all of the volumes in the Christian Initiation series: *The church is the context of Christian formation.* That is not to say that God's grace does not reach people outside of the church. United Methodists believe that God's *prevenient* grace "goes before" people as God beckons them through Jesus Christ. It also does not mean that only church members will be saved. No Scripture warrants that kind of arrogance!

Rather, the idea means that the church is the place where people experience God in the community of the body of Christ. It is the context in which the "means of grace" (Wesley's phrase for practices like worship, Bible study, prayer, fasting, and so forth) make sense. The church is far more than a voluntary society. It is nothing less than a living reality, the continuing life of Christ on this earth, in the power of God's Spirit.

To say this about the church is also to recognize that the church is human. It is composed of fallible beings who struggle against sin. At the same time, the church is a vessel filled with a treasure. Through the church God offers the gospel of life and peace and holiness to the world. The church humbly and gratefully proclaims the righteousness and holiness of the God of Israel to the world. In this book we will try to keep both the fallibility and the treasure of the church in view as we talk about how the church is the context for formation.

Jesus commanded the infant church to *make* disciples (Matthew 28:19). Jesus knew that Christians have to be formed, fashioned, shaped, made, and molded in the church—the community that is the ongoing life of Jesus Christ in the world. Of course, God is the one who saves. Nothing we do can save anyone. But God is also the one who has chosen to act through human beings in a special way through the church. God calls the church to be a sign of the faithful love and saving work of God. In this community, people are forged into witnesses of God.

Tertullian, an early North African Christian said, "Christians are made, not born." As far as the statement goes, it is true: no one becomes a Christian through natural childbirth.

But the statement can also be reversed: Christians are birthed in water and the Spirit, not made. They are given birth by God, in the church. Protestants have usually avoided using early Christian references to "Holy Mother Church." Yet there is a sense in which the phrase is true. Christians are not born to new life in Christ on their own, but rather they come to birth in and through a community of believers.

It is for these reasons that *Come to the Waters* insists that Christian initiation is the ministry of the entire congregation. (See pp. 25-42.) It is a *shared* ministry to which all members contribute in their own way. Each member formally and informally contributes to the formation of new Christians in many ways. Living as examples of faithful discipleship is the most important contribution members can make to the formation of initiates. Nobody is perfect. Therefore, faithfulness, not perfection, is the virtue we hope to present to people interested in becoming Christians.

As catechist, you have a special role to play in the initiation process; you coordinate the task of formation—in formational group sessions, in worship services, and in other ways to be discussed in the chapters that follow—through the four stages of inquiry, formation, intensive preparation, and integration.

Before we discuss the details of your task in the initiation process, let's discuss who a catechist is.

WHO IS A CATECHIST?

1. WHAT DOES THE WORD "CATECHIST" MEAN?

The term "catechist" is new for United Methodists, yet the ministry itself goes back to the days of the early church. A catechist is a layperson or a member of the clergy who has responsibility for forming initiates to the Christian faith through the pilgrimage to baptism and beyond.

Why use the term "catechist"? For me, the word utterly captures the multi-faceted ministry performed by this person. The term *catechist* derives from the Greek root *echo*. A catechist is one in whom the Word of God "echoes" and one who seeks to help others "resound" with the Word of God.

However, the critical issue is the ministry, not the word naming it. Even though this resource uses "catechist," "catechumen," and "*catechesis*," you and your congregation should not feel bound by these terms. If you and your congregation choose to use other terms (such as "formation director" for catechist, "initiate" for catechumen, and "formation" for *catechesis*), that is perfectly acceptable.

2. WHAT KIND OF A PERSON IS A CATECHIST?

Catechists help form and develop the faith of those who come to the church seeking God. They do this by embodying what it means to be a Christian in thought, word, and practice. They make the Christian faith visible in a way that enables people to learn discipleship. By their practice catechists can show initiates that it is possible to live the life to which they feel called and that the way of discipleship is filled with joy—in spite of the costs, risks, and sacrifices along the way.

As a catechist, you serve as a living "icon," a flesh-and-blood representation, of Christian discipleship. You serve not as a "finished product," not as a model to be patterned after (not even John Wesley claimed to have achieved perfection in love), and not as an all-wise sage. Instead, you serve as an example of humanity made alive to God through Christ in the Holy Spirit. You model for initiates the truths that you speak about in the formational group sessions.

The best teachers are usually those who show their students that they have not yet "arrived." Likewise, catechists have discovered that we are all perpetual beginners. Thus, catechists can relate to newcomers and respond to them with compassion and wisdom, even while they demonstrate to these initiates what it means to be a good learner.

As a catechist, you will guide initiates through the different stages of Christian initiation. Because you know the stages that mark the way, you can act as a guide, but at the same time you are a companion. Exemplify the reality that the life of discipleship is never completed. The people of God are pilgrims who are always on the journey.

People who enter the catechumenate (the process of Christian initiation) can take comfort in the fact that they are never alone on the pilgrimage; they are joined by the community of faith, which is marked by the sign of Christ.

WHAT DOES THE CATECHIST DO?

For the catechist, the ministry of forming disciples is based on the method of "experience followed by reflection" (*CTW*, pp. 60-61). This means that you will help initiates reflect on Scripture and on the Christian faith, as well as help them form and nurture relationships with God, with you, and with the congregation. The heart of this method is the "[c]ontinuous reflection on Scripture and the experiences of prayer, worship, gifts for ministry, and ministry in daily life…" (*CTW*, p. 61). However, reflection always follows experience. Indeed, the goal of Christian formation is for initiates to experience God's call in Jesus Christ and to respond to that call through faithful discipleship.

Leading initiates to desire and experience God's transforming call on their lives is a delicate art. It means helping people develop a taste for the affections of the heart and practices of the mind and body that make Christian life what it is. Your ministry as catechist is not simply a matter of teaching people some prayers to say in the morning or of showing them how to read Scripture in a new way. It involves whetting people's spiritual appetites for the nourishing "food" of the Word. We are used to the equivalent of "spiritual junk food." It is not easy to switch from a diet of froth to one of substance.

As a catechist, you help people realize their spiritual hunger and help them recognize that only God's nourishment can satisfy their needs. You also show them how they can be immersed in the culture (i.e., beliefs, practices, and world views) in which this nourishment makes sense: the culture of the family of Christ, the church.

1. THE CATECHIST AS GARDENER

Comparing forming disciples to the labors of a gardener (see 1 Corinthians 3:5-9) provides helpful insights into the nature and scope of your ministry as catechist. My wife and I began to garden in earnest this summer. As we turned the heavy clay soil of our yard, added compost, and tried to grow a variety of plants, my mind dwelled again and again on the work of a catechist. Here are some ways in which your ministry is like the work of a gardener:

- *Successful gardening takes planning.* A gardener must have a clear idea of the contents of the garden and how to lay it out to accommodate the plants in the best possible way. Likewise, formation in the Christian faith takes planning. You, the pastor, the sponsors, and other members of the Christian initiation leadership team know the objectives, structures, and stages of the initiation process outlined in *Come to the Waters.* Plan the content of the process in a way that will be formative for each initiate. Become familiar with the entire sweep of Christian initiation, from the seeker's first inquiry to the last post-baptismal gathering of the newly-baptized.

- *A gardener knows the plants in a garden.* She or he knows whether a certain flower likes acidic or alkaline soil and whether a specific ground cover likes shade or sun. A gardener knows how long it takes for each plant to grow to full maturity. In the same way, a catechist understands that each person is unique and that discernment and care is necessary when relating to initiates. A catechist relates to the individual needs and situation of the person seeking life in Christ. This sensitivity to the history, personality, and issues each person brings to the process of formation is essential. The catechist, along with the pastor, sponsors, and the entire faith community, helps each person discern when the time for baptism has come. The initiation process often includes people who have been baptized (perhaps as infants or as children) but who want to reaffirm their baptism. It may also include youth who are preparing for baptism, or for the first public affirmation of their baptism—a process that since 1964 has been called "confirmation." The catechist is sensitive to the special challenges and requirements that the formation of these people may present.

- *A gardener knows the "pests" that lurk in a garden and how to deal with them.* She or he knows where and how to look for the first signs of infestation or disease. Similarly, a catechist knows that the journey of Christian initiation is full of potential detours and dangers that could divert an initiate from the way. In close cooperation with the pastor, the sponsors, and the other members of the initiation leadership team, the catechist works to bring initiates through times of difficulty.

- *A gardener knows how to feed plants.* She or he knows what each plant needs and how much food to give at one time. For example, a good gardener knows that too much nitrogen stimulates leaf growth but thwarts fruitbearing. The gardener also knows that the excessive application of fertilizer can burn young plants. In a similar way, a catechist attempts to nourish initiates in a measured way that strengthens without causing burnout.

- *A gardener is patient and diligent.* Gardening does not reap immediate rewards, at least not in terms of fruit and flowers. To be successful, a gardener has to be out in the garden every day, watering, feeding, protecting, staking, and pruning the plants. She or he knows that if there is to be a chance of seeing fruit or flowers in the future, the gardener must work hard in the present. Likewise, a catechist will be diligent, seizing any teachable moment. A catechist will be available to address the questions and concerns of initiates. Also, a catechist will be patient with initiates without being condescending. Christian initiation is not like a factory, which mechanically and instantly produces a product. It is a process that unfolds at a pace that is designed for individual initiates. Some may enter the inquiry phase and live there for months, or even years, as they try to discern God's will. Others may decide immediately after the first period of inquiry that they want to be baptized. The key is to help each person discern (without coercion) when she or he is ready to move to the next stage.

Comparing your ministry to gardening may create the impression that if you work hard enough, are diligent enough, and do the right things, success is guaranteed. Gardening does not work that way and neither does Christian formation. No matter how much work a gardener may put into the garden, she or he ultimately discovers that this work is merely in cooperation with the mysterious process of life itself, over which there is only limited control.

As you labor in the "garden" called the church, working to nurture and cultivate new "plants" (initiates) so that they will bear fruit, remember that *formation is God's work, not ours.* God is ultimately responsible for the birth and formation of disciples. Catechists merely cooperate with the mysterious process of disciple making. God is not limited by our timetables or by what we in the church do.

At the same time, God has promised to be with us. We can trust God's promise to give Godself in the sacraments we celebrate. Indeed, in the sacraments God is the one who acts first. We can be confident that our mission of making disciples is a faithful response to Christ's call and, therefore, it receives God's blessing.

The success of Christian formation or *catechesis*, then, does not depend exclusively on us and on our activity. Our work is that of faithful friends. We are not workers who expect a certain wage and who end the day angry because the God who hires freely also gives freely. (See Matthew 20:1-16.) We work as catechists in the hope that what we do may be counted as some of the leaven of the reign of God, which acts secretly, quietly, and in ways utterly beyond our control.

2. THE CATECHIST AS MENTOR

Let's further specify the relationship between the catechist and initiates by comparing it to the relationship between a master and an apprentice. (See *CTW*, p. 100.)

As masters, catechists are mentors. Mentoring relationships stand at the heart of formation. Newcomers learn what it means to be a Christian through their relationships with members of the community of faith and with each other. In this network of relationships, two are of particular importance: that between the initiate and the catechist and that between the initiate and her or his sponsor(s). *Accompanying the Journey* describes in great detail the relationship between initiate and sponsor, so we will not discuss it here. Let's focus instead on your role as a mentor to the initiates.

You are like a master craftsman (or craftswoman) who teaches by doing. Your apprentices (the initiates) come to you to learn about your craft (the Christian faith and life) by watching you at work and by receiving hands-on instruction in the craft. Apprentices develop a relationship with you, and you with them. As a mentor, you teach them more than just the mechanics of the craft. You teach them how to *be* people who are proficient and experienced in their craft. You form them in the behaviors, attitudes, and views of the world that are part of your craft.

Of course, the metaphor goes only so far in matters of Christian faith and practice. You do not have to be perfect or feel that you have reached a particularly lofty level of Christian life to be a good mentor. The important element in the metaphor is not that the craftsman is masterful in the craft, but rather that there is a formative relationship between craftsman and apprentice.

At the same time, it *is* important that you embody the faith you proclaim. The mentor-apprentice relationship is formative because the mentor gives the apprentice an example to observe, to follow, and to question. So there is a sense in which you need to be visibly walking in the way of discipleship. There is also an important teaching principle at stake here: The more familiar you are with Christ's way, the more you will be able to speak about it with the voice of experience.

Being a mentor has everything to do with relationships. Catechists need to be aware of the many kinds of relationships (and their contexts) in which initiates find themselves as they make the journey to baptism. The relationship between you and the initiates is important, but only insofar as it helps you guide people preparing for initiation. You are there to help people form relationships with God and other Christians.

WHERE DOES FORMATION HAPPEN?

As a catechist, where does your ministry happen? It takes place in two settings:
- the congregation, as it participates in the rhythms of the initiation journey, and its liturgical life
- a small group within your congregation, called a formational group.

In this section, we discuss both settings. We begin with an overview of the structure of the initiation process as a whole and then move to a discussion of the formational group setting. We also look briefly at the place of discernment in the initiation process.

1. THE NECESSITY OF A STRUCTURED PROCESS

One of the biggest obstacles to overcome in your ministry is a resistance to using a structured process of Christian initiation to help the church make new Christians. There is a certain distrust of ritual in mainline Protestant denominations. In the United States of America, Protestant worship has tended to distance itself from the fixed prayers and structures of worship. Set prayers stifle the Spirit, so the argument goes; having rituals tends to lead to faith in the ritual itself, rather than in God. If we believe this, why bother having a process of initiation at all? Why not simply live and let live, allowing people to come to faith as they will, when they will, and how they will?

This view is based on a misunderstanding of the process of initiation. There is considerable freedom in the initiation process; the church does not dictate that inquirers have certain experiences or learn a predetermined amount before taking the step to become hearers. Even when a person makes the decision to join the catechumenate, the process of formation has been deliberately left open-ended. The hearer, the catechist, the pastor, the sponsor(s), and the community of faith together exercise discernment about when it is time to take the "next step" of intensive preparation for baptism. Thus, there is much flexibility in the process of Christian initiation.

But the process of Christian initiation needs both structure and flexibility. The structure for Christian initiation, as outlined in *Come to the Waters,* takes two forms:
- *Stages*: inquiry, formation, intensive preparation, and integration
- *Services of Initiation*: special services celebrated at the threshold of each stage

The use of a process marked by stages is not meant to suggest that the church is trying to make the religious experience of all Christians conform to the same model. Instead, stages make visible to the initiate and the entire community the authentic, life-changing transition that coming to faith and deciding to be baptized entails. Even though the experience of coming to faith may happen instantaneously for some people, the Christian community has always recognized that the life of discipleship involves, as it were, leaving one country and making the long journey to another, as Abraham did when he heard and heeded God's call (Genesis 12). The use of ritual has been and continues to be one way in which the church helps people negotiate the transitions in their lives, including the transition to a life of faith in Christ. The rituals of Christian initiation (the stages and services) point to and participate in the deeper realities of conversion at the heart of the process of coming to faith.

As catechist, you are deeply involved in the rituals of the initiation process—the stages and the services. You guide and accompany initiates in the special services the church celebrates with initiates. You also preside at some services; we will discuss later how you can do this.

The point is that you are present at each stage of the process, and at each service you are with the initiates, celebrating the transition from one stage to the next.

Let's review the basic stages and threshold celebrations (*CTW*, pp. 34-35).

Figure 1
Stages and Services of Christian Initiation

Stage One: Inquiry
- happens as part of the church's ministry of evangelization
- brings people into the church for intentional questioning about life of faith

Goal: inquirer decides to become a hearer

Service of Initiation: A Service for Welcoming Hearers (*CTW*, pp. 109-112)

Stage Two: Formation
- hearer engages in worship; reflects on Scripture, prayer, and ministry in daily life through an approach called "experience followed by reflection" (*CTW*, p. 60-61)

Goals: (1) hearer grows in her or his ability to "discern God's activity and call in…daily life;" (2) mutual discernment shows hearer to be ready for baptism

Service of Initiation: A Service for Calling Persons to Baptism (*CTW*, pp. 113-115)

Stage Three: Intensive Preparation
- takes place during Lent or Advent
- candidate engages in examination of life; reflects on Scripture leading to baptism, congregation prays for candidate, candidate accompanies congregation toward baptism

Goal: candidate is initiated with baptism at Easter or on Sunday celebrating the Baptism of the Lord

Service of Initiation: Holy Baptism (*CTW*, p. 120; the services of "Baptismal Covenant I" are found in *UMH*, pp. 33-39, and *UMBOW*, pp. 86-110, and the service for the Easter Vigil is found in *UMBOW*, 369-376.)

Stage Four: Integration
- newly-baptized enters "more fully into the life of the community of faith"; reflects on the meaning of initiation, on ministry of the church, on the sacraments, and on the life of discipleship; participates in "discernment of spiritual gifts and clarification of ministry in daily life"

Goal: newly-baptized begins a lifetime of faithful discipleship

Service of Initiation: A Service for Affirmation of Ministry in Daily Life (*CTW*, pp. 120-121)

2. DISCERNMENT

Discernment is a key element in the pilgrimage from inquiry to baptism and to integration in the body of Christ. It helps answer the question: Where do we—the initiate, the sponsor, the catechist, the pastor—go from here?

Discernment is the prayerful, open listening for God's voice at the times when the church needs to make decisions. Individual Christians also use discernment in making decisions. They may prayerfully meditate on Scripture, turn to wise and trusted friends, or seek the counsel of a pastor or priest.

We can trust that the Spirit dwells in the church and continues to speak to the church. Thus, in the process of discernment the Christian community can rely on the Spirit's help.

In the case of Christian initiation, discernment involves prayerful, centered listening to many voices: Scripture, the initiate, the pastor, the deacon(s), the sponsor(s), the catechist, and the congregation. We trust that in listening to these voices, we will hear the voice of the Spirit.

Discernment typically happens at the thresholds of the initiation process as inquirers become hearers, as hearers become candidates for baptism, and as the newly-baptized discern God's call as they discover their vocation and gifts for ministry.

Initiates truly need discernment as they struggle with the threshold question or set of questions connected with each stage of the initiate's journey. (See *CTW*, pp. 101-103.) Inquirers ask: "Do I want to pursue this journey toward life in Christ further and with this group of seekers and experienced Christians?" Hearers ask: "Am I called to become a living member of the body of Christ through baptism?" Candidates ask: "Am I ready to renounce evil, repent of my sin, and confess Jesus as Savior and Lord at baptism?" The newly-baptized ask: "How will I follow Jesus under the guidance of the Holy Spirit? What is my calling? What are my gifts for ministry in the world and in the body of Christ? What do I need from other Christians to persevere in a life of loving God and serving others?" The formational group is the setting for these and other questions.

This process of discernment must necessarily be open-ended and free to follow the Spirit's leading. It cannot follow a rigid formula. At the same time, some structure and discipline is necessary for the voices of Scripture, the initiate, the pastor, and the sponsor(s) to be heard.

It is impossible to outline a model for discernment since initiates and congregations are unique. Yet we can say that Scripture, prayer, service, listening, and conversation are indispensable elements in the process.

There is a growing number of resources in the area of discernment. I suggest you begin with the discussion of discernment in *Accompanying the Journey* (pp. 46-51).

3. THE FORMATIONAL GROUP

Leadership and size of the group

The local congregation is the basic form of Christian community. Small groups are another type of Christian community within the congregation; membership in small groups can be crucial for growth in the faith. Both kinds of community are important for your ministry. Indeed, centering Christian formation in a small-group setting returns United Methodists to a very Wesleyan practice. The use of small groups, called "class meetings," for Christian formation was one of the hallmarks of the Methodist movement in John Wesley's day and beyond.

The formational group you will lead provides a primary context for the shaping of new Christians preparing for baptism and for integration in the life of the congregation. Each initiate joins a formational group for the purpose of sharing experiences, receiving biblical and spiritual guidance, and joining in prayer. You lead each formational group with the help of other experienced Christians who are sensitive to the questions and needs of the initiates.

Preferably, formational groups should meet weekly. A small number of initiates may require only one group; a large number of initiates may need more than one. I recommend that formational groups have no more than seven members. More than seven makes it difficult to have the kind of interaction necessary for formation.

It is advisable that each formational group be led by two catechists, especially if the group is made up of both male and female initiates. Two catechists allow for shared leadership and broadened perspectives.

Structure and content of group sessions

Because of the great diversity within The United Methodist Church, it would be foolish to impose rules about the structure and conduct of formational groups, or what the exact content of the sessions should be.

There is no single method that will be right for all people at all times. In general, people seem to learn more when teachers and mentors rely not on one mode of teaching and learning but use a combination of approaches. This is particularly true in matters of the faith, where a didactic approach (that is, a lecturer conveying information to a class) will fail to speak to the whole person for whom the gospel is intended. As *Come to the Waters* (pp. 60-61) points out, "experience followed by reflection" is a much better way to engage the truths the Christian community strives to see embodied in inquirers, hearers, and candidates. This method reflects how we hope Christians will learn throughout their lives.

Although there is no *single* pattern or structure to *catechesis*, I also believe that whatever form *catechesis* takes, there will be some constants in its process and content. The Roman Catholic educator James Dunning has suggested that there are key ingredients to the process of formation. Consider incorporating these ingredients into the structure and content of formational group sessions:

1. *Let there be story-telling.* All people have stories to tell, especially those embarking on a journey of faith, conversion, and healing.
2. *Let there be questions.* All people come to the process with questions about the meaning and purpose of life, about God and human beings and how they are related to each other, about the church and the community. Such questions are the windows through which our own stories and questions are connected to the Christian story and to God.
3. *Let there be a community of faith.* Stories and questions are shared in a community of peers—sponsors, congregation members—who share their faith and prayer companions. Further, there is a community of faith that gathers for worship.
4. *Let there be tradition.* Tradition is the story the community has to tell, accounts of personal journeys with God from Abraham and Moses to Bishop Tutu and Mother Teresa. We hand on this tradition first through the lectionary, the great story of our faith, and then through the lives and written records of Christians through the centuries.
5. *Let there be conversion.* At the very center of the process is the story of Jesus, the one who was crucified, died, and rose again. The catechumenal process allows space and time for this dying and rising, this transformation so familiar in our lives, to be given new meaning. In Christ, people can share their brokenness and find healing and new life. In Christ they can "risk the conversion process."

6. *Let there be celebration.* The catechumenal process "restores the integral ties between cat-echesis and liturgy, word and rite." These rites need to be celebrated with lively signs, with colorful sights, and with the smells and sounds of liturgy.
7. *Let there be mission.* "At rock bottom, the Catechumenate journey is the Church's way of forming people for mission." The Great Commission is acted out in the lives of candidates as they dare to journey to the font; but it is also lived out as they begin their own ministries of service in Christ's name.[1]

The ingredients of formation that Dunning mentions support the formational approach of "experience followed by reflection" recommended by *Come to the Waters.* This approach also draws on "[s]torytelling, worshiping, doing the word in service to the poor and suffering, discovering opportunities for service in daily life, and reflecting on Scripture" (*CTW*, p. 61) to form faithful Christian disciples.

According to *Come to the Waters*, the key elements around which guidance and reflection happen in formational group sessions are the congregation's *worship, public and private reading of Scripture, prayer,* and *ministry in daily life* (p. 55). To make this possible, each formational group session has two parts:

• listening for the Word of God in the weekly lectionary readings, which are considered in light of the initiate's ongoing life of prayer, worship, and ministry in the world
• raising and answering questions about formational issues that may emerge, such as learning the content of Scripture, acquiring spiritual disciplines, and learning some church history (*CTW*, p. 55)

To ensure that both of these parts are adequately covered, include at least the following elements in each formational group session:

• a maximum of seven people
• leadership by a catechist(s) and other experienced Christians
• provision for mutual accountability in discipleship
• opportunities for sharing experiences of conversion and growth in discipleship
• opportunities for hearing and reflecting upon God's Word
• opportunities for spiritual guidance
• opportunities for regular prayer
• opportunities for reflecting on ministry in the church and in the world

There are, of course, a wide variety of ways to structure the formational group sessions. Use your creativity under the guidance of the Holy Spirit. To help you get started, consider the outline for a formational group session in Appendix One (p. 76); study also the outline found on pages 154-155 in *Come to the Waters.*

Formation and the stages of initiation

Come to the Waters recommends that formational groups be formed as early as the inquiry stage and continue through the integration stage. This ensures that engagement with the congregation's worship, prayer, ministry in daily life, and Scripture takes place along the full spectrum of the initiation process.

It is crucial that catechists have a thorough understanding of the stages and services of initiation. It is particularly important that you study the "threshold questions" (*CTW*, pp. 101-103) that initiates will consider at the different stages of formation. Under your guidance, group members will consider the questions pertinent to each stage (inquiry, formation, intensive preparation, and integration) within the context of the life each person is beginning to lead: one shaped by prayer, worship, Scripture, and ministry in daily life in Christ's name.

To provide background material and practical suggestions for the content of the formational group sessions, and to help you integrate the sessions with the stages of the initiation process, this book is organized in the following way: the central chapters of the book focus on the basic elements of the formational group sessions: Scripture (Chapter Two), worship (Chapter Three), prayer and disciplines (Chapter Four), and ministry in daily life (Chapter Five). Moreover, each chapter provides discussion and helpful hints for how the topic of the chapter (for example, Scripture or worship) may be approached and integrated at all four stages of the initiation process.

Scripture, worship, prayer and the disciplined life, and ministry in daily life are important, sustaining provisions for the pilgrimage of initiation and lifelong discipleship. For people coming to conversion and new life in Christ, a good part of the journey involves learning how to use the provisions God has given for the journey.

The provisions of Scripture, worship, prayer and disciplines, and ministry in daily life are really "means of grace" (a good Wesleyan term). We can think of the process of Christian formation as learning how to use the means of grace for the lifelong journey of discipleship, not simply for the short-term goal of admittance to the church. As a catechist, you have wonderful opportunities through the formational group sessions to model the means of grace and to help initiates incorporate them into the rhythms of their daily lives.

TO WHOM DOES THE CATECHIST RELATE?

In the process of initiation, catechists relate to the whole congregation—for example, through participation in the special services. You are also part of a team of leaders. (See *CTW*, pp. 53-56 for a discussion of the different roles and ministries in which these leaders participate.) Two of these leaders are especially important to your ministry as catechist: the pastor and the sponsor.

1. THE CATECHIST AND THE PASTOR

By now you may question the boundaries between what the pastor does and what the catechist does. To be honest, this can be a touchy matter requiring sensitivity, discernment, and respect on the part of catechist and pastor alike.

At the outset, we need to keep in mind that formation is the entire congregation's responsibility. No one person, whether it be the pastor or catechist or someone else, can possibly replace the faith, practice, and ministry of an entire Christian community. Thus, every individual ministry of Christian initiation needs the context of the entire church.

At the same time, United Methodists and other Christians believe that the ordained ministry has been given by God for the building of the church and that elders and deacons have been given specific responsibilities in the church. "Service, Word, Sacrament, and Order" is how *The Book of Discipline* describes these responsibilities. (See ¶ ¶ 301-303.) Elders have the responsibility for proclaiming God's Word in preaching and teaching, for administering the sacraments, and for ordering the life of the church for mission and service, as legislated by General Conference and written in the *Discipline.* Deacons also have specific responsibilities in connecting the church's work with its service in the world. Moreover, licensed local pastors lead many United Methodist churches.

Where does your ministry as catechist fit within this structure? There is no easy answer. That is why it is essential for the whole Christian initiation leadership team to talk through expectations and presuppositions about roles and responsibilities.

At your gathering, the team may wish to consider these questions:

- As we read Scripture and *The Book of Discipline*, what is our understanding of ministry in the church and in the world?
- How is authority exercised and shared in this ministry?
- What models in Scripture may help us clarify what God wants us to be as a team as we perform this ministry?
- What style or styles of ministry do we want to embody? Should our ministry be primarily hospitable? safe? nurturing? challenging? contemplative? healing?
- How do we best communicate with each other and coordinate our ministries and roles together as we assist the congregation in its journey with people toward baptism and integration?

2. THE CATECHIST AND THE SPONSOR

Catechists and sponsors share the ministry of formation. Perhaps the main difference between your ministry as catechist and that of the sponsor is the context in which each ministry happens. You are responsible for the formation of initiates *as a group* in the context of formational group sessions. Sponsors are responsible for the formation of *individual* initiates in the context of personal relationships that involve both the activities of the church (including the formational group) and daily life outside the church.

Thus, catechists and sponsors work together for the formation of initiates. What initiates encounter and learn in formational group sessions, they explore, assess, and try to live out with the assistance and support of their sponsors. To illustrate this relationship, let's borrow a metaphor from *Accompanying the Journey*, comparing the process of Christian initiation to that of learning a foreign language. As Lester Ruth suggests, the sponsor provides a safe environment where the grammar and vocabulary of the new language called "Christian" can be tried without fear of awkwardness or embarrassment (*AJ*, pp. 37-38). Through her or his relationship with the initiate, a sponsor reinforces, elaborates, and deepens what the initiate learns about Christian "grammar" and "vocabulary" in the formational group sessions and in the experience of worship and ministry in the world.

It is very important that catechists and sponsors work together. As a catechist, you can assist sponsors in their ministry by encouraging them to attend formational group meetings. You may also provide the sponsors with an outline of the content of the formational group sessions. In addition, you and the sponsors should meet on a regular basis to discuss the initiation process and discuss the effects of the group sessions in the initiates' formation.

Besides being partners in formation, sponsors are invaluable sources of feedback; they have a unique perspective on the initiation process that you need to hear.

In each chapter I will outline ways in which catechists and the sponsors can work together toward your common goal of forming lifelong, committed disciples.

A FINAL SUGGESTION AS YOU BEGIN

If a gardener puts too much nitrogen-rich fertilizer on a young plant, it will produce lots of green leaves but no flowers or fruit. The overabundance of nitrogen stimulates short-term growth of a particular kind, but it does the plant little good in the long run. Similarly, if you try to load initiates with lots of wonderful practices and knowledge, you may have a positive, short-term response; but too many practices to master and too many insights to incorporate often overwhelms initiates. They are unable to put down deep, strong roots.

As you read this book and consider the ways to carry out your ministry, you may be tempted to do too much at one time. In my own experience as a teacher, I have discovered that there are times when trying to do too much with a class leads to frustration on the part of students and exhaustion and burnout on the part of the teacher. Choose instead a limited number of practices and subjects for your formational group to assimilate over time.

To assist you in making these choices, I have listed a goal statement for each of the chapters that follow. Furthermore, in each chapter, the sections discussing the four stages of initiation (inquiry, formation, intensive preparation, integration) contain practical suggestions to use with initiates in formational group sessions and outside these sessions. I hope that structuring the discussion in this way will help you plan your formational group's experience wisely.

RESOURCES

This book presumes that you have access to the other volumes in the Christian Initiation series, all published by Discipleship Resources:

Benedict, Daniel T. Jr. *Come to the Waters: Baptism & Our Ministry of Welcoming Seekers & Making Disciples.*

McDonald, William P. *Gracious Voices: Shouts & Whispers for God Seekers.*

Felton, Gayle C. *By Water and the Spirit: Making Connections for Identity and Ministry.*

Ruth, Lester. *Accompanying the Journey: A Handbook for Sponsors.*

Below are other resources about the process of Christian initiation (the catechumenate) that provide valuable reading:

Edwards, Tilden. *Spiritual Friend: Reclaiming the Gift of Spiritual Direction.* Mahwah, New Jersey: Paulist Press, 1997.

Office of Evangelism Ministries of The Episcopal Church. *The Catechumenal Process: Adult Initiation and Formation for Christian Life and Ministry.* New York: The Church Hymnal Corporation, 1990. See especially pp. 105-128 and Appendix C.

Farnham, Suzanne G., et.al. *Listening Hearts: Discerning Call in Community.* Harrisburg, Pennsylvania: Morehouse Publishing, 1991.

Friends Conference on Discernment. Richmond, Indiana: Earlham School of Religion and Quaker Hill Conference Center, 1985. A valuable collection of essays on the practice of discernment.

Hill, John W.B. *Making Disciples: Serving Those Who Are Entering the Christian Life.* Toronto: The Hoskin Group, 1991. See especially Parts Two and Three, which discuss *catechesis.*

Jones, Alan. *Exploring Spiritual Direction: An Essay on Christian Friendship.* Minneapolis: Winston Press, 1982.

Matthaei, Sondra Higgins. *Faith Matters: Faith-Mentoring in the Faith Community.* Harrisburg, Pennsylvania: Trinity Press International, 1996.

Westerhoff, John H. III, and O.C. Edwards. *A Faithful Church: Issues in the History of Catechesis.* Harrisburg, Pennsylvania: Morehouse Publishing, 1981.

Chapter Two

SCRIPTURE

Give us this day our daily bread. (Matthew 6:11)

What is the goal of Scripture in formation?

To form inquirers, hearers, candidates, and the newly-baptized into people who have a taste for the food God gives through God's Word in Scripture.

Your ministry as a catechist revolves around Scripture. It is your primary source. The Word of God is food for the heart, a rich feast. It is so important to formation that we can say that the essence of formation is the encounter between people and the word of God in Scripture. This may sound daunting. The Bible is often difficult to interpret; even scholars disagree about its meanings. How can a lay catechist hope to sufficiently present the Bible to those seeking to become Christians?

The good news is that your ministry does not involve teaching an extended Bible study course. Your job is to help make possible an encounter between the word of God in Scripture and the questions and life issues that people bring to their journey of formation. You are helping to open the initiates' ears to the living voice of God in Scripture as it is embodied in the life of the church.

But you may be thinking, "The Scriptures were written so long ago. How can they speak to us today?" They do because both testaments contain the story that forms Christians, a story that interprets our lives in *its* terms, not our own. Initiates are not primarily learning the history of Scripture. Instead, inquirers, hearers, candidates, and the newly-baptized view their life stories in light of the story of God's saving love, which remains steadfast even in our faithlessness and our sin. The church invites the initiates and the newly-baptized to respond to God's faithfulness as the Scriptures reveals it in their own lives.

Recall that there are four stages to the baptismal journey: inquiry, formation, intensive preparation for baptism, and integration. At each of these stages people encounter the word of God in the Scriptures of both the Old Testament (Hebrew Bible) and the New Testament.[2] Because each stage has its unique questions, the encounters with Scripture will be different at each stage. The goal of formation is not to use the Bible in a mechanical way or to treat it as a magical book with which to divine answers to life's mysteries. Rather, Scripture serves as a mirror in which inquirers, hearers, candidates, and the newly-baptized view themselves and their questions in light of God's will, as revealed in the history of Israel and the life, death, and resurrection of Jesus Christ. Once the fourth stage of the journey (integration) has begun, the Scriptures will serve as a life-long companion.

Initiates and the newly-baptized will encounter Scripture in the context of its use in the church. The Revised Common Lectionary provides a way for the church to read and hear the Word of God in three separate yet interrelated communal contexts: the celebration of the birth, ministry, death, and resurrection of Jesus Christ in the liturgical year; the weekly celebration of the Lord's Supper, the thankful memorial of Christ and his saving work; and the weekly "breaking of the bread" of the Word in the sermon.

These communal contexts of memorial, celebration, and proclamation nourish and inform the individual reading, hearing, and meditation on the Word. Thus, part of your ministry in the formational group sessions will involve helping people learn how to encounter God's Word in these settings. Therefore, the Sunday lectionary readings will be the focus for the discussions, questions, and meditations for the weekly formational group. (*CTW*, pp. 73 and 75-77, discusses the readings for Lent, Years A, B, C; they are particularly appropriate for use during the intensive preparation stage.)

Next, we will discuss briefly some of the issues surrounding the role of the Scriptures at each stage of the baptismal journey. As with all of the materials in this book, the following observations and suggestions are not rules but guidelines and spring-boards for creativity.

SCRIPTURE AND THE INQUIRY STAGE

At this point in the journey, people have responded to the invitation of the Spirit to actively consider entering the process of Christian initiation. As *Come to the Waters* says, "During this period, believers supported by their leaders help inquirers to discern the answers to the questions, 'What are you seeking? What is happening in your life that prompts your search?'" (p. 104). These questions are to clarify for seekers the dynamics in their lives that have led to their search for belonging, for love, and for meaning; they also help focus the goal of the search on a relationship with God in Christ.

1. THE IMPORTANCE OF THE SUNDAY SERVICE

For mainline Protestant denominations, the Sunday service remains one of the chief means by which seekers are first exposed to the faith. Here seekers encounter the word of God through the reading of Scripture and psalms, the hearing of sermons, and the singing of hymns.

The Word of God is "bread" for all who are starving spiritually. It is critical that the reading and singing of Scripture be done with care so that inquirers may truly encounter God's Word. In too many churches the reading of Scripture is hurried or performed as if the readings were "lessons" to be endured. The reading of the Word of God in the Sunday service is a potentially life-changing event. Scripture deserves to be read in a way in which people (particularly inquirers) will listen.[3]

The person who reads Scripture in the Sunday service differs from congregation to congregation. Some United Methodist congregations have a liturgist; others have a reader (or readers). In others, the pastor, the deacon, or the diaconal minister reads. The reading should be treated as an important, transformative event, regardless of who reads it. Good reading is not primarily a matter of liturgical good taste; it is about evangelism.

2. The Importance of a Formational Group

Come to the Waters (p. 104) suggests that small groups may be formed to bring inquirers together for weekly discussion. Formational groups can be excellent settings for inquirers to address, in light of Scripture, the questions that clarify their search for belonging, for meaning, and for love. In formational groups inquirers can ask experienced Christians, such as catechists and sponsors, to address these issues.

The Scriptures hold up to questioning. In fact, they are filled with questions: Some are put forth by God to Israel; others are put forth by Israel to God; and others are put forth by individuals to one another. Questioning is a two-way process: Inquirers question God's Word, and through the Word, Christ asks them, "Who do you say that I am?" Both dimensions are important.

Formational groups provide inquirers with a space to ask questions. They also show that the church takes each inquirer seriously and treats her or his questions with respect. Respect implies an openness to the variety of life contexts that prompts inquirers' questions. The last contact with a Christian community many contemporary people have had was in childhood and adolescence. Others have been wounded by the church. Many know a lot about world religions but have not committed to following any of the ways they have encountered or studied. Some come to the church after their spiritual pilgrimages have led them from one religious community to another. Others seek God out of the deep needs of their lives.

As the ones who lead the formational group sessions, catechists need to be sensitive to the variety of life experiences and reasons for seeking God that inquirers bring.

3. Ways to Use Scripture with Inquirers

Help your congregation's worship committee think about how Scripture is read in the Sunday service(s). Consider how the reading can be conducive to enabing an encounter between inquirers and the Word of God. Suggest organizing a class designed to improve public readings of Scripture. As a catechist, you do not have to be responsible for planning or leading such classes. However, one of your jobs may be to point out the importance of these classes when the leadership team plans the process of Christian initiation for your congregation.

In formational group sessions, ask people to view their own life stories in light of biblical encounters with God. Instead of trying to find passages from the Bible that you think will address inquirers' questions, it may be better to focus on the stories of Jesus encountering people. Such stories give inquirers a framework within which to ask questions about what brings them to their search.

Consider these stories of Jesus:

Luke 19:1-10
Luke 24:13-35
John 4:1-42
John 9:1-41

In formational group sessions, discuss the weekly Scripture readings for Sunday worship from the Revised Common Lectionary. As they encounter the Word of God, ask inquirers to consider the following questions in light of the biblical witness: "What place does faith have in your life? Are you ready to reorder your life in order to hear and follow the call of Jesus Christ? Are you willing to do this by making a disciplined exploration of Christian living and service to God and neighbor?" (*CTW*, p. 104).

SCRIPTURE AND THE FORMATION STAGE

Once an inquirer has decided to enter the journey toward baptism and life in the church, the reading, hearing, and contemplation of Scripture become central in her or his life.

"A Service for Welcoming Hearers" in *Come to the Waters* makes clear the relationship between formation and the Word of God. At the point in the service when the inquirer makes her or his first public acceptance of the gospel, she or he is asked: "Will you listen to the Word of God and open your heart and mind to welcome Jesus as your Lord and Savior?" The inquirer responds, "I will, with God's help" (*CTW*, p. 110).

Later in the service, the hearer (after this service the inquirer is known as a hearer) is invited to hear the Word of God:

God's Word is like bread for our hearts; we cannot live without it. God's Word is like rain that comes down upon the earth, bringing forth fruit in our lives. Come and be with us as a hearer of the Word of God. Let the Word of God guide your way and bring you to everlasting life (*CTW*, p. 112).

Afterwards, the sponsor presents a Bible to the hearer while the catechist says:

Receive the good news of Jesus Christ, the Son of God. Read and listen for the voice of Jesus, the living Lord. Listen to hear, trust, and follow him (*CTW*, p. 112).

The service firmly sets formation in the context of the Word of God; it establishes the hearer's task and also the agenda for your ministry as catechist.

1. THE BOOK THAT READS ME

During the formation stage, catechists, sponsors, and the congregation help hearers discern answers to the two threshold questions of this stage: "Do you desire to be baptized?" and "Do you desire life with the church?" Reading Scripture assists hearers, catechists, and sponsors to test "the depth and perseverance" of the hearers' desire "to explore life as a Christian and to live as a disciple" (*CTW*, p. 102). The period of formation is the time for hearers to search their hearts as they allow the Word of God to challenge, question, and shape them.

How can hearers read the Scriptures to discover answers to their questions, particularly the threshold questions? Two elements are necessary for this kind of reading: prayer and ongoing participation in the community of the church.

Prayerful reading of Scripture places the hearer in a position to be receptive to the voice of Christ. By prayerful reading I mean that the reader, who has taken a moment before to quieten inner thoughts, is open to the prompting of God as she or he reads from the Scripture. Maintaining an inner quiet takes discipline and practice. At first hearers will find it hard to quieten their inner thoughts, but with time and patience the quiet will come. (In the next section I discuss an ancient form of prayerful reading of Scripture called *lectio divina*.[4])

Participation in the church community provides another context for hearing and discerning the living Word of God. The church's life embodies the gospel in relationships of love. Reading Scripture while actively living out the gospel is crucial for discovering its meaning for our lives. Without ongoing participation in the church's life, our interpretation of and reflection on Scripture will be incomplete at best; at worst, our interpretation and reflection will be skewed to our own limited views and understandings of the gospel.

In addition, by reading Scripture from the context of participation in a congregation, hearers will be able to answer the threshold questions of the formation stage from a perspective that is realistic about the life of the church. Hearers will see the church as it is, both good and bad. As they contemplate baptism and life with the church, hearers will be fully aware of the faith community's strengths and weaknesses.

2. LECTIO DIVINA: "CHEWING" ON THE WORD

Reading and listening as hallmarks of understanding Scripture

Read, listen. Hear, trust, and follow Christ: The service for welcoming hearers identifies these as the hallmarks of the encounter with the Word of God during the formation stage. Employing the *lectio divina* way of reading Scripture will help hearers make these hallmarks an integral part of their lives. *Lectio divina* literally means "divine reading"; it refers to the practice of prayerful, contemplative reading under the guidance of the Holy Spirit.

Lectio divina involves a slow, prayerful, and meditative reading of the week's lectionary passage (or one of the Gospels) in light of the threshold questions from the formation stage. *Lectio divina* has been used by Christians for centuries to hear God's voice in Scripture.

Let's look at the two central actions of *lectio divina*: reading and listening. The service for welcoming hearers could have told the hearers as they receive the Scripture, *learn* to "[r]ead and listen for the voice of Jesus..." (*CTW*, p. 112). Even though American society boasts a relatively high rate of literacy, we should never assume that all seekers and hearers can read and that those who can will know how to read Scripture in the way implied by the service. Nor can we assume that we have mastered the art of listening—especially the listening required to hear the voice of God.

How we read the things in our lives depends largely on context. For example, do you read a paperback novel in the same way that you read a letter written by someone you love? Scripture can also be read through different lenses, depending on what is being sought. A biblical scholar may read Paul's first letter to the Corinthians for clues about the structure of early Gentile Christian communities. A preacher may read the same text and find background for a story about an early congregation struggling to be faithful.

Similarly, hearers will read Scripture with the relevant threshold questions on their minds and hearts. Moreover, hearers bring questions reflecting their social, economic, and racial-ethnic perspectives to the reading of Scripture.

These differing outlooks will always be present when hearers are reading and discussing Scripture. In formational group sessions catechists must be sensitive to these as they help hearers make the connections among Scripture, their experiences, and the journey of formation.

Catechists should also be aware of and sensitive to how their own contexts have shaped their viewpoints and lives. By being aware of your own blind spots, you will help the initiates, and they will help you.

Using lectio divina in formational groups

The ancient practice of *lectio divina* is an excellent way for formational groups to encounter the Word of God. (See the outline for formational groups found in Appendix 1 of *Come to the Waters* [pp. 154-155]; it incorporates a form of *lectio divina*.)

The practice of *lectio divina* works in this way: A group (or an individual) reads a passage of Scripture aloud and spends time reflecting on and praying through the passage. Members of the group then share insights. The process is repeated two or three times. Afterwards, someone concludes the time together with prayer.

The idea behind *lectio divina* is that Scripture is our spiritual "food" and that we need to "break open" the Word for it to nourish us. Ancient Christian authors, for example, often interpreted the petition of the Lord's Prayer, "Give us this day our daily bread," to mean the bread of the Word. In *lectio divina*, we ruminate on—"chew on"—the bread of God's Word.

Note the construction of the petition from the Lord's Prayer: "give us" acknowledges that the bread we seek is God's to give; "this day" shows that we need God's nourishment daily. In Exodus 16 God provided manna from heaven, but there were restrictions: It had to be collected in the morning, and God would not allow it to be hoarded. Similarly, God gives us the Word day by day, requiring that we not be anxious for the future (Matthew 6:25-34).

Lectio divina is a communal practice, whether one does it in a group or alone. When we pray the Lord's Prayer, we ask not for "*my* daily bread," but for "*our* daily bread." We make our petition as part of a community, for a word from God that is meant for each member of the community of faith.

The amount of Scripture read does not have to be lengthy. Your formational group will probably focus on no more than one of the lectionary readings (preferably the Gospel reading) for the week. When hearers practice *lectio divina* at home, they may read only a verse or two before a particular word or phrase strikes their attention, and then they enter into prayer. At other times, the opposite may be true: a lengthy reading captures their attention and prompts prayer.

Which Scriptures should hearers read? I suggest that they read the passages given for weekly Sunday worship from the Revised Common Lectionary. (Be sure to follow the appropriate year, Year A, B, or C). Studying the lectionary readings will automatically link the hearers' formation with the Scriptures heard, read, and prayed about by the rest of the congregation. Moreover, using the lectionary ensures that hearers encounter both the Old Testament and the New Testament. Another possibility is for your formational group to read one of the Gospels during the course of your meetings.

You should know that using the Revised Common Lectionary in your sessions is not necessary. Adjust the readings if the formational group needs to hear and pray through a different Scripture passage (or passages) from the one given in the weekly lectionary readings. If you do this, though, I urge you to make the lectionary Scripture readings the usual group readings since they link the hearers with what the rest of the congregation hears in worship.

SCRIPTURE AND THE INTENSIVE PREPARATION STAGE

Of course, using the practice of *lectio divina* for reading and reflecting on Scripture should not be limited to the formation stage; it should also be used during the intensive preparation and integration stages of the process of initiation.

As candidates prepare for baptism during the days of Lent or Advent, the lectionary Scripture passages (particularly the Gospel readings) shape the contours of their journeys. The Gospel readings speak of blindness and enlightenment, human disbelief, and the power of Jesus' word to heal and to raise people from the dead. The passages speak of turning from evil and turning to Christ and of entering into death trusting in Christ. (See *CTW*, pp. 75-77.)

During the intensive preparation stage, the catechist's goal in the formational group sessions is to help candidates make connections between the Gospel texts and the threshold questions the church will ask at baptism: "Do you renounce the spiritual forces of wickedness, and repent of your sin? Do you confess Jesus Christ as Savior and Lord?" (*CTW*, p. 102). *Come to the Waters* outlines one way of integrating reflection on the Gospel readings with intensive preparation for baptism (see *CTW*, pp. 76-77).[5]

Another way to help candidates make connections among the threshold questions, Scripture, and their upcoming baptisms is to use the Apostles' Creed as a framework for experience and reflection. As will become clear below, the Creed involves all four dimensions of the congregation's life: worship, prayer and the disciplines, ministry in daily life, and Scripture. We discuss the Apostles' Creed in this chapter on Scripture, though, because the Creed is a particularly apt summary of the story of salvation as narrated in Scripture.

Handing on the faith of the church

One of the crucial encounters with the Apostles' Creed during the period of intensive preparation is a rite called "Handing on the Faith of the Church" (*CTW*, p. 116). During this service, which may take place on the third Sunday in Lent (or Advent), the congregation "hands on" the Christian faith to the candidates by reciting the Apostles' Creed; catechists may also present each candidate with a copy of the Creed as a keepsake and for continued reflection during the remaining weeks of Lent.

Candidates will have encountered the Creed by the time the congregation shares it. Because the Apostles' Creed is the *church's* creed, there is a sense that candidates cannot receive it until the formal congregational rite. Encourage candidates to view this moment as an important step along the road of discipleship.

According to *Come to the Waters,* handing on the Apostles' Creed is vital to the candidate's preparation for baptism, for it

> ...connects Christians with their ecumenical heritage and links them to the apostolic faith and witness of the early church. As a baptismal creed, it serves as the basis for entrance into the baptismal covenant and helps the candidates to relate diverse scriptural texts to the essential narrative of God's saving action (p. 116).

The Apostles' Creed is like a road map in that its words provide Christians with the symbols of their faith pilgrimage. These symbols also connect individual Christian journeys to the larger map of the Christian story through the centuries. The Creed condenses the wisdom of nearly twenty centuries of Christian pilgrimage and serves as an important ecumenical center of faith.

At the same time, the Apostles' Creed should draw us into the experience of faith. Creeds originated in the baptismal practices of early Christians. Thus, they belong in the realm of praise as much as in the realm of doctrine. That is, when we confess our faith in the context of the baptismal service and in the Sunday service, we engage in a specific type of worship of God.

(1) Using the Apostles' Creed in formational group sessions

The Apostles' Creed is a doorway for candidates to contemplate the relationship between their emerging faith in Christ, their upcoming baptisms, and their daily lives. The Creed stimulates reflection on what many Christians through the centuries have affirmed as central elements of the faith. In formational group sessions, catechists may help candidates experience how the simple clauses unlock the wealth of several centuries of thought. *Gracious Voices* includes a wide selection of witnesses to each clause of the Apostles' Creed. (See *GV,* pp. 29-80.) Selections from *Gracious Voices* could easily form the foundation of your formational group's reflection on the Creed.

As a way to connect insights from the Apostles' Creed to their daily lives and to their experience of the ecumenical church, candidates may consider questions such as these:
- What does it mean to call God "Father"? How do your experiences of being a parent and your recollections of relating to your parents shape how you understand this clause? How should we address God today in a way that does not alienate people of either gender?
- Why does the Creed mention Jesus' suffering? What does Jesus' suffering have to do with the suffering we and others experience in our lives?
- The Creed calls the church "catholic." This term means "universal" or "whole." How does racism prevent the church from being catholic? What can we do to make the church more catholic?

The important thing to remember is that you do not need to conduct a seminar in Christian theology as the group discusses each part of the Creed. The focus is on Christian living and the upcoming baptisms of the candidates.

Indeed, as *Come to the Waters* says, the Apostles' Creed serves as the basis for the candidates' entrance into the baptismal covenant. It helps them connect a variety of passages from Scripture "to the essential narrative of God's saving action" (*CTW*, p. 116). The central question the formational group should ask of each part of the Creed is: What has this part to do with my life as a living member of the body of Christ? In addition, consider discussing the following questions as a way to help candidates connect the Apostles' Creed and the lectionary Scripture readings to the meaning of their baptisms:
- "Do you renounce the spiritual forces of wickedness, and repent of your sin?" (*CTW*, p. 102)
- "Do you confess Jesus Christ as Savior and Lord?" (*CTW*, p. 102)
- "What must change (die) in you in order that Christ's reign of love and justice may flourish in your life?" (*CTW*, p. 106)
- "How will you live for Jesus in your daily life?" (*CTW*, p. 106)

To ensure that you cover all of the Apostles' Creed during the six weeks of Lent, consider using the following schedule:
- Weeks 1-2: God the Father; Creation
- Weeks 3-4: Jesus Christ
- Weeks 5-6: Holy Spirit; Church; Last Things

(2) Handing on the Apostles' Creed with integrity

As is the case with all of our liturgical gestures, there must be a positive relationship between the rite and the life of the congregation for it to have integrity. For example, the practice of racism in the church makes a mockery of the baptismal practice and the church's welcome to all who love the Lord. Racism denies the equality of all people as they are baptized into Christ, and it makes the invitation to Communion an empty, hypocritical act.

In a similar way, if the Apostles' Creed does not form a regular part of the church's life, teaching, and mission, the gesture of handing on the Creed will be empty and even hypocritical. How, then, do we make the Creed an important, regular part of congregational life? Ask the pastor and members of the initiation leadership team to consider the following possibilities:

- Reciting the Apostles' Creed regularly in worship (as a response to the Word) brings before all members the character of the Creed as a confession of the apostolic faith.
- Reaffirming the baptismal covenant (see *UMH*, pp. 50-53) regularly helps establish the connection between the Apostles' Creed and baptism.
- Including references to the appropriate clauses of the Apostles' Creed in a variety of "teaching moments" stimulates congregational reflection on the meaning and relevance of the Apostles' Creed for discipleship today.

Perhaps the most difficult yet most critical link to establish is one between the Apostles' Creed and the congregation's life of service and mission. Western Christians seem to have lost the ancient sense that creedal affirmations have immediate consequences for how Christians live and act in the world as members of the body of Christ. This development has meant that, even when United Methodists have recited the Creed, they have seen it as a dreary bit of verbiage to get through on the way to the pastoral prayer or the choral anthem.

By making the Apostles' Creed an integral part of congregational worship and by studying it in formational group sessions, catechists may play an important part in connecting the Creed with members' (and candidates') baptisms and with the congregation's life and mission. In this way, the act of "handing on" the Creed will have integrity.

(3) Memorizing the Apostles' Creed for use in daily life

Candidates may find memorizing the Apostles' Creed valuable. For centuries, Christians have memorized Scripture (the Psalms, significant verses), prayers (the Lord's Prayer and others), hymns, and creeds. Memorization is still a valuable practice today. Many Christians can attest to the strength they have derived from being able to recall a meaningful verse of Scripture or prayer as they have confronted trouble or need.

Memorization is different from learning by rote. The latter simply stores information for later repetition. Memorization, on the other hand, allows a person to have access to information for use in daily life. A memorized text, prayer, hymn, or creed is available for contemplation. Over time, such texts become part of us, woven into the fabric of our very selves.

Texts can be memorized in a variety of ways. The most tedious, of course, is to repeat a text or write it out enough times for it to be memorized. A better way is to integrate the text into one's daily prayer. For example, the order for an individual's morning prayer as contained in *The Book of Common Prayer* of the Episcopal Church in the United States of America suggests that the Apostles' Creed be said before one prays for others and for oneself (p. 137). Another possibility is to set the text to a simple tune for use in the Sunday service. (See *CTW*, p. 93). Repeated use of the Creed will gradually fix it in the mind.

SCRIPTURE AND THE INTEGRATION STAGE

Integration is the fourth stage of the initiation process and also the most difficult, for the flow of the process creates a natural climax at the time of baptism. There could easily be a letdown after Easter (or Baptism of the Lord Sunday)—a sense that the job is "done." Thus, the task of catechists and the congregation is to continue the momentum of the initiation process. The journey for all, both the newly-baptized and experienced Christians, has just begun.

The integration stage lasts the seven weeks of the Season of Easter and reaches a peak at Pentecost (or the remaining weeks after Epiphany, which reaches a peak on Transfiguration Sunday) when the congregation celebrates and affirms the ministry, witness, and gifts of all its members (including the newly-baptized) for ministry in the world. "A Service for Affirmation of Ministry in Daily Life" (*CTW*, pp. 120-121) takes place on Pentecost Sunday (or Transfiguration Sunday) and may follow the structure of "An Order for Commitment to Christian Service" in *The United Methodist Book of Worship* (pp. 591-592).

During the integration stage, the newly-baptized discover that they are a part of a sacramental community, and they discern their gifts for ministry and prayerfully consider God's call to find places of service in the congregation and in the world.

As the newly-baptized ponder their gifts and places of service in light of the upcoming service, consider using these threshold questions as a way to focus formational group discussions:

- "How will you endeavor to follow Jesus Christ under the guidance of the Holy Spirit?"
- "What is your sense of calling?"
- "What support do you need from other Christians in order to continue as Christ's faithful disciple?" (*CTW*, p. 103)

You may connect reflection on the threshold questions with prayerful thought about Scripture in the following ways:

- Meditate on the questions in light of the Gospel readings in the lectionary for each Sunday of the Season of Easter (or the Sundays after Epiphany).
- Reflect on the questions in light of Ephesians or 1 Peter; both epistles dwell on baptismal themes.
- Contemplate the questions in light of passages from both the Old Testament and the New Testament that testify to the renewing, healing, and sanctifying power of the Holy Spirit.[6]

At this point in the process of initiation, it would be very appropriate to include the newly-baptized in the ministry of reading the Scriptures during the Sunday service. Such participation makes visible the relationship between the read Scripture (the word of God in the Bible) and Jesus Christ (the living Word of God) who gives new life to those who turn in faith to God.

If you wish to pursue this option, talk with your pastor and/or the chairperson of the congregation's worship committee to discuss how it could be done. No pressure should be put on the newly-baptized to participate in public reading; but you may be surprised at how many people sign up.

SCRIPTURE AND MINISTRY WITH THE POOR AND MARGINALIZED

This ministry provides a necessary context for reading and reflection on the Scriptures, especially for affluent Christians. It makes initiates aware of their own context and aware of how that context shapes (and sometimes distorts) the way they understand and use Scripture. Ministry with (never service *to*) the poor and marginalized may challenge, and perhaps even correct, the initiates' interpretation of and approach to Scripture. In such a ministry we serve Christ who identified with those in need (Matthew 25:31-46), and Christ ministers to us.

If your church operates a soup kitchen or weekly meal program, service in that setting (including working with and talking with the people who come to eat) can shed light on what ministry in Christ's name means. This idea applies to any ministry in which hearers, candidates, and the newly-baptized engage.

Helping initiates make the connection between their ministry with the poor and the marginalized and with their reflection on Scripture is an important dimension of the catechist's task—not only during the integration stage but also during the formation and intensive preparation stages.

SCRIPTURE, FORMATION, AND THE SPONSORS

In their role as encouragers, sponsors may foster the practice of *lectio divina* and the practice of reflecting on Scripture in light of ministry with the poor and the marginalized. By giving initiates a copy of the Bible (as *Accompanying the Journey*, p. 22, suggests), sponsors signal that they take seriously the role of Scripture in the initiate's formation. During the week, sponsors and initiates can practice together *lectio divina* or another way of meditating on Scripture.

In their role as guides and companions in the process of initiation, sponsors are in the position to frequently talk with initiates about the questions and insights they have formed from their encounter with God's Word. This kind of conversation helps stimulate the initiate's ongoing reflection.

RESOURCES

Crockett, Joseph V. *Teaching Scripture from an African-American Perspective.* Nashville: Discipleship Resources, 1990. Provides a model that employs four distinct strategies of education: story, exile, sanctuary, and exodus. Contains a valuable chapter on "Teaching Scripture with Cultural Specificity."

Hauerwas, Stanley. *Unleashing the Scripture: Freeing the Bible from Captivity to America.* Nashville: Abingdon, 1993.

Jennings, Theodore W. *Loyalty to God: The Apostles' Creed in Life and Liturgy.* Nashville: Abingdon, 1992.

Robins, Wendy S. *Through the Eyes of a Woman: Bible Studies on the Experience of Women.* Revised edition. Geneva: WCC-World YWCA Publications, 1995.

Turn to God - Rejoice in Hope. Bible Studies - Meditations - Liturgical Aids. Geneva: WCC Publications, 1996. Originally prepared as a guide to preparation for the eighth assembly of the World Council of Churches in Harare, Zimbabwe, held in 1998. This resource embodies an ecumenical use of the Scriptures, combining scriptural passages, meditation, and worship. Part II, "Meditations," could easily be used by inquirers or hearers, and Part III, "Lenten Liturgical Bible Studies," would be especially appropriate for candidates during the intensive preparation stage.

Weber, Hans-Ruedi. *The Book that Reads Me: A Handbook for Bible Study Enablers.* Geneva: WCC Publications for the World Student Christian Federation, 1995. Contains creative approaches to unlocking the Scriptures' ability to speak to, judge, and challenge contemporary people. Chapter 5, "Meditation on the Bible," is especially useful for catechists.

Chapter Three

WORSHIP

O come, let us sing to the LORD;
let us make a joyful noise to
the rock of our salvation! (Psalm 95:1)

What is the goal of worship in formation?

To form inquirers, hearers, candidates, and the newly-baptized into people whose lives are offerings of praise and worship to God, both in the church and in the world.

This chapter answers three related yet different questions:
- What is the catechist's role in the special worship services for inquirers, hearers, and candidates?
- How can the catechist relate worship to formation at each stage of the process of initiation?
- What does worship have to do with formation and with the ministry of the catechist?

The first and second questions deal with practical, nuts-and-bolts issues. The third is a more theoretical question that has practical implications. The first two questions can be answered quickly and easily; the third will take more time, and the issues it raises will be of interest not only to you but also to your pastor and worship committee.

WHAT IS THE CATECHIST'S ROLE IN THE SERVICES OF INITIATION?

As I mentioned in Chapter One, there are special services that take place at threshold moments in the journey to baptism and, subsequently, to full integration into the life of the church. Catechists participate in the leadership of these services, along with the pastor, sponsors, and representatives of the congregation.

Figure 2
The Catechist's Role in the Services of Initiation

STAGE ONE: INQUIRY

Service of Initiation: "A Service for Welcoming Hearers" (*CTW*, pp. 109-112)

Part 1: Greeting
   Welcomes inquirers and invites them to stand before the people.

Part 4: First Acceptance of the Gospel
   Assesses the willingness of inquirers to attend worship faithfully, receive direction as disciples, listen to God's Word, and welcome Jesus as Lord and Savior.

Part 5: Commitment of Sponsor and Congregation
   Assesses the commitments of the sponsor and the congregation to care for inquirers and to assist them in knowing God and following Jesus Christ.

Part 7: Invitation to Come and Hear the Word of God
   Invites hearers to receive the good news of Jesus, to read and listen for the voice of Jesus, and to hear, trust, and follow Jesus. May present each hearer with a *Hymnal*. (See p. 40 in *Echoing the Word*.)

STAGE TWO: FORMATION

Service of Initiation: "A Service for Calling Persons to Baptism" (*CTW*, pp. 113-115)

Part 1: Presentation
   Presents hearers to the pastor and congregation. *(If the newly-called candidates leave the service to meet in a formational group, the catechist accompanies them.)*

STAGE THREE: INTENSIVE PREPARATION

Service of Initiation: "Holy Baptism" (*UMH*, pp. 33-49)

   Catechist may participate by laying hands upon candidates and extending acts of welcome and peace.

   During intensive preparation, three rites are offered prior to baptism:

   Rite: "Handing on the Faith of the Church" (*CTW*, p. 116)

   Led by presider and catechist. Catechist may give each candidate a copy of the Apostles' Creed.

   Rite: "Handing on the Prayer of the Church" (*CTW*, p. 117)

   Led by presider and catechist. Catechist may give each candidate a copy of the Lord's Prayer.

   Rite: "Examination of Conscience" (*CTW*, pp. 117-119)

   Led by presider and catechist.

STAGE FOUR: INTEGRATION

Service of Initiation: "A Service for Affirmation of Ministry in Daily Life" (*CTW*, pp. 120-121)

   Role of catechist may be decided in consultation with pastor and initiation leadership team.

As you can tell from the service for welcoming hearers, catechists have an important part to play at the beginning of the hearers' journey of formation. As a catechist, you ask inquirers to accept the gospel for the first time. You call for the sponsors and the congregation to be committed to the formation of the new hearers. You invite hearers to hear the Word of God with the congregation in worship and in formational group sessions.

The service for calling persons to baptism indicates the catechist's important role at the beginning of the period of intensive preparation. In the service, you have the happy job of presenting the hearers to the pastor and congregation as candidates for baptism. Your ministry with the candidates is by no means finished at that point. In fact, some of the most intensive formational group sessions await. Rather, in a sense you are handing back to the church those who were given over to the process of formation when they became hearers. You are bringing a major stage of the process full-circle.

If your pastor wishes, you may also help lead the rites of "Handing on the Faith of the Church" (third Sunday in Lent or Advent), "Handing on of the Prayer of the Church" (fifth Sunday in Lent; the Sunday after Christmas), and "Examination of Conscience" (third, fourth, and fifth Sundays in Lent; third and fourth Sundays of Advent and the first Sunday after Christmas).

A case can be made for either the pastor or the catechist leading these rites. The pastor's leadership symbolizes the church's faithfulness to the gospel through the centuries. The catechist's leadership symbolizes the close connection between the Apostles' Creed, the Lord's Prayer, and the experience of formation. The pastor and catechist may lead these three rites together and, thus, combine both symbols.

Your presence in the services of initiation and the rites is truly important; your gracious, well-prepared, and unhurried participation in these serves the entire initiation process.

WORSHIP AND FORMATION

Worship is often the first place where people seeking faith in Christ experience the gospel and its life in the church. In this age of mainline denominational decline, we are more acutely aware of the profound impact of worship on people seeking God and God's righteousness. In this section, we explore the relationship between worship and formation. We will spend time talking about theory before we move to practice because so much change is happening in worship today. We need to talk first about the "big issues" related to how Christians worship, and what that has to do with formation.

If you are a catechist who is a layperson, you may be asking, "What does all of this have to do with me and my ministry?" After all, your work as catechist happens primarily in the formational group and its activities, not the Sunday service. Besides, you may think, "In The United Methodist Church, isn't the pastor responsible for thinking about and organizing worship?"

The reason I include this extended discussion is because the church's worship has too great an impact on formation to ignore. Moreover, for the process of Christian initiation to fully embody the gospel, the entire initiation leadership team—including you, the catechist—must be concerned with the role of worship in the process of initiation. Even if the plan and organization for Sunday services and for festivals are left to the pastor and worship team, it is still useful for you to understand how worship can form initiates at each stage of the process.

1. HOW WORSHIP FORMS CHRISTIANS

First, let's talk about a theology of worship. Christian worship tells the story of salvation in Christ. Through hymns, psalms, readings, sermons, prayers, confessions, and sacraments, the church proclaims the good news of salvation in Christ. Through the Christian Year the church follows the ministry of Christ from his birth and baptism (Advent-Christmas-Epiphany) to his death, resurrection, and giving of the Spirit (Lent-Easter-Pentecost). (See *CTW*, pp. 71-85, for more about the connection between worship and the Christian Year.)

In worship we are repeatedly confronted with the good news that the sin that separated us from God has been defeated by Christ, whom God raised from the dead for our salvation. We experience through words, gestures, water, bread, and wine the love of God who calls us to conversion and to the restoration of God's image in us.

God's gifts to us form only one aspect of worship. In worship we reach out with loving words and gestures. We speak words of forgiveness, we exchange signs of peace, we welcome one another in the name of God, we anoint, and we give Communion. Thus, we can say (using an inadequate spatial metaphor) that there is a *vertical* and a *horizontal* dimension to our worship. Both are necessary, yet both are open to distortion.

To emphasize the vertical dimension of worship at the expense of the horizontal is to neglect or even to forget that the transcendent God is also immanent, is wholly other, but also nearer to us than our own breath. To emphasize the horizontal dimension at the expense of the vertical is to turn worship into a sentimental, folksy event that is centered on us rather than the God who gathers the body of Christ.

2. A DIFFERENT WAY OF LOOKING AT WORSHIP

Worship forms us because participation in common actions and in common prayers molds certain Christian dispositions in us. This formation through actions and words happens whether we are aware of it or not; however, we need to become conscious of it. The catechist and pastor (primarily but not exclusively) are responsible for asking the question about the congregation's worship, "Is what we are doing positively or negatively formative, especially as it affects initiates exploring the faith?"

What does it mean for worship to be "positively or negatively formative"? Perhaps an example from my own experience will best illustrate what I mean. When I was fifteen, I attended a weeklong Christian summer camp with classes for children, youth, and adults. I eagerly attended a class entitled "Worship in Spirit and Truth." For a week I heard the teacher (a visiting professor) speak profoundly about worship reform and renewal in the local church.

The culmination of the class was to be a love feast held on the final night of the camp. That evening I climbed the hill leading to the clearing at the summit where the love feast would happen. After we sang hymns, read Scripture, and heard a sermon, the officiant told us to form small groups for fellowship. I knew no one at the event. As the small groups formed, I tried to make eye contact with anyone who might let me into a group. After a few minutes of trying to enter a small group, I quietly walked back to the main camp.

I learned more about worship in spirit and truth that evening than had been intended. I tell this story to share an instance of the power of worship to alienate as well as include, to form negatively or positively.

Worship has perhaps the greatest impact on the formation of people new to the faith than any other thing the church does. Thus, worship will be a central element of the process of formation prior to baptism. To say this means that we must confront the liturgical diet of our congregations to see how Christians are "fed" in our worship. We must pay close attention to what our worship says to seekers, to hearers, and to candidates. In my experience at the love feast, the actions of the people were not consistent with the words spoken during the week and at the love feast. This danger is as old as Christianity itself, as Paul's letters to the Corinthian church attest. (See especially 1 Corinthians 11:17-25.)

WORSHIP AND THE INQUIRY STAGE

To talk about worship at the inquiry stage places us in a minefield of contemporary debate about what worship is all about. For many seekers and inquirers, the experience of worship can be the deciding factor in choosing a church. Recognizing this, many authors have suggested a range of ideas for making worship attractive.

Often, the first thing these authors suggest is to do away with "traditional" worship. The reasons for this proposal are clear. The Sunday service as practiced by mainline Protestant congregations has tended to be non-participatory, clergy-dominated, short on Scripture, long on verbose prayers, and marked by a style seemingly more interested in decorum than in worshiping the God of Jesus Christ. Bluntly put, worship is often considered just plain dull!

Certainly, there is much to criticize. Yet, it seems to me that behind the advice to throw out "traditional" worship in favor of "contemporary" services lies a misunderstanding of what traditional Christian worship is really all about. The pattern of Sunday worship among today's mainline North American Protestants emerged as a result of many factors, including nineteenth-century revivalism; the spread of Christianity across the western frontier; a lack of ordained clergy to officiate at the sacraments on a weekly basis; and an Enlightenment rationalism that saw no need for sacraments. By the Civil War, many denominations normally worshiped on Sundays with a service designed more for the conversion of non-Christians, not the weekly nurture of Christians through praising God, hearing God's Word, and receiving God's transforming, nourishing grace in the Lord's Supper.

By traditional worship I mean something altogether different. Traditional worship as I understand it is deeply rooted in the experiences of Christian life over the last twenty centuries. This experience is diverse and, at the same time, bound together by an ancient *common structure* known to Christians since the second century, if not earlier.

This common structure, rooted in Jewish synagogue worship and domestic worship practices, contains two parts: (1) the reading and proclamation of the Word of God, and (2) the celebration of a meal of bread and wine, over which thanksgiving to God has been offered. Prayer for the world and the church provides the hinge between the two parts. The structure is truly that simple. The diversity of the tradition exists because Christians worship according to this pattern but in a variety of cultures and time periods.

Perhaps the problem with mainline Protestant worship is that it is not traditional enough! In terms of the ongoing life of Christians who continually need to hear the call to repent and to receive God's grace, the traditional mainline Sunday service provides a thin diet. This is not to deny that the Methodist people have adapted to this diet in the two centuries of their existence. The question today is whether that diet is sufficient to sustain and nourish a people that is called to be conformed to the image of God in Christ and to be sent into the world to proclaim the good news of life in Christ. The answer to this question goes to the heart of Christian formation. The experience of the mainline denominations for the past thirty years provides a resounding "No!" People want and need more than that kind of service can provide. On this issue most agree; the disagreement emerges over the question of *what* people want and need.

One of the gifts of the liturgical movement of the twentieth century has been the reclamation of the Word-Lord's Supper pattern of Sunday worship. (See *UMH*, pp. 2-5, and *MV*, pp. 2-4, for an example of worship both new and ancient, participatory, and rich in Scripture and sacrament.) This manner of worship provides the food United Methodists need for today's life and mission. In other words, United Methodist worship will once again provide nourishment at the two "Tables" (as they were known in early Christianity): the Table of the Word and the Table of the Lord's Supper.

Today's society suffers from a spiritual famine. People are seeking God in different places, except it seems in Christian communities. From this fact alone, one can conclude that mainline Protestant worship has lost touch with the lifestyles and inclinations of seekers of a certain generation. If you believe this conclusion, you may suggest that worship should adopt the musical styles, language, and customs of the contemporary culture.

It seems to me that the problem with this solution is that it assumes that people (especially seekers and inquirers) want more of what their culture already offers (or bombards them with) every day. This solution assumes that Christian worship must speak the language of contemporary culture for it to be understood.

This assumption raises four fundamental questions:

(1) What is contemporary culture? Does this culture comprise a single whole?

(2) If contemporary culture is indeed a single entity, is its language the only one Christians should be able to speak in worship?

(3) Is it really true that people today can understand only the language of contemporary culture?

(4) Are people today really looking for worship that mirrors the contemporary culture?

The answers to these questions could fill a book. However, two brief comments must suffice. First, the problem with a sole reliance on the language of contemporary culture in Christian worship is that it provides no link with preceding Christian communities. It fails to even provide a connection with other Christian communities of the present. A connection with the past is crucial, for our identity as Christians derives from the faith communities that preceded us. Second, it seems to me that people do not want yet another venue presenting the contemporary culture. They do not want the mall; they want God!

The riches of Christian tradition can provide the resources for a nourishing, sustaining, creative spirituality today, if only we will reclaim it. This will be difficult because the language of the gospel is so different from what we are accustomed to speaking and hearing.

All of this implies that the renewal of United Methodist worship will be central to the success of Christian formation. By renewal I mean reforming the congregation's main Sunday service to bring it in line with the norm specified by *The United Methodist Hymnal*: a weekly service in which the Word of God is amply heard and fully proclaimed; a service in which the church prays for others and itself; a service in which the church gathers around the Table to receive the body and blood of Christ; and a service in which the church is sent out in mission to the world in the name of Christ.

As you think about your work with inquirers, consider the following suggestions:

- With the pastor, the worship committee, and the initiation leadership team, consider how your congregation's worship could better reflect the good news of Jesus to inquirers. You may begin by reviewing Chapter Seven in *Come to the Waters* (pp. 87-98).
- In formational group sessions:
  Ask inquirers to share their views about how your congregation's Sunday worship helps (or fails to help) them prepare to answer the threshold question: "What do you seek?" In what ways do the worship services help inquirers connect their longings and their stories with God's story? (See *CTW*, p. 101.) Reflect together on the meaning of the "Basic Pattern for United Methodist Worship" found in *The United Methodist Hymnal* (pp. 2-5).

WORSHIP AND THE FORMATION STAGE

During the formation stage, hearers engage in and reflect on a variety of activities. Participating in the congregation's worship is a particularly important activity for hearers. What the congregation does and says in its weekly worship is a rich resource for formation.

The goal of the congregation's worship during the formation stage is to provide settings that allow hearers to assess the depth of their desire to live as Christians in the body of Christ through baptism. Eventually, hearers will respond to the threshold questions: "Do you desire to be baptized? Do you desire life with the church?" (*CTW*, p. 102)

For congregations using the "Basic Pattern of Worship," the text of the Sunday service (both words and actions) will be a central resource for the formation stage. Even if your congregation does not follow the "Basic Pattern," I suggest that you use the texts found in *The United Methodist Hymnal* (pp. 2-5) or *Mil Voces Para Celebrar* (pp. 2-4) when you refer to United Methodist worship practices. Refer to them in conjunction with the actions, patterns, and texts of worship in your own congregation.

Why rely so heavily on what *The United Methodist Hymnal* or *Mil Voces* has to say about worship? The answer is simple: For more than two hundred years, Methodists have understood that the *Hymnal*—"a little body of experimental [i.e., experiential] and practical divinity," as John Wesley called it—is second only to the Bible in terms of being the key devotional and theological text. Today United Methodists are fortunate to have all the materials needed for corporate and individual worship life in one book. (See Figure 3 on p. 40.)

In addition, *The United Methodist Hymnal* (and *The United Methodist Book of Worship*) have been approved by the General Conference. In other words, the body authorized to speak for The United Methodist Church has said, in effect, that these books embody the tradition of United Methodist worship today. They carry considerable weight in deliberations about the form and content of United Methodist worship.

Furthermore, the way the hymns are arranged in *The United Methodist Hymnal* or *Mil Voces* provides a wonderful framework for your formational group's reflection on what it means to be a United Methodist Christian, and for its reflection on the love, mercy, and transforming power of God through Christ in the Holy Spirit. Singing some of the classic Charles Wesley hymns about conversion, justification, and sanctification could be a weekly beginning point for deep conversation and reflection on what it means to be called by God, saved by God, and made holy by God's Spirit.

Figure 3
**Worship Resources in *The United Methodist Hymnal*
and *Mil Voces Para Celebrar: Himnario Metodista***

Services of Word and Table I-IV (*UMH*, pp. 6-31; *MV*, pp. 6-17)
Services of the Baptismal Covenant I-IV (*UMH*, pp. 32-54; *MV*, pp. 18-29)
Seasonal Prayers (scattered throughout both resources)
An Order for Morning Praise and Prayer (*UMH*, pp. 876-878; *MV*, pp. 64-65)
An Order for Evening Praise and Prayer (*UMH*, pp. 878-879; *MV*, pp. 64-65)
Affirmations of Faith (*UMH*, 880-889; *MV*, pp. 68-71)
Prayers of Confession, Assurance, and Pardon (*UMH*, 890-893; *MV*, p. 170)
The Lord's Prayer (*UMH*, 894-896; *MV*, p. 130)

Should you also use *The United Methodist Book of Worship* as a resource? I think the *Book of Worship* works best as a secondary resource. Most United Methodists will not encounter the *Book of Worship* on a regular basis.

The *Book of Worship* is an excellent guide to United Methodist practice, and it provides liturgical options supplementing the worship resources of the *Hymnal*. It should be consulted when questions arise about United Methodist worship today, and people preparing for baptism need to be made aware of the riches it contains. However, claim the *Hymnal* as the primary liturgical resource for the formation of Christians in the United Methodist tradition. It is the worship book hearers need to know.

Several suggestions about how catechists may use the resources of the *Hymnal* during the formation stage follow:

1. THE HYMNAL IS A GIFT

The *Hymnal* is such an important resource for the formation of hearers that it would make an excellent gift. This act could easily be integrated into the service for welcoming a hearer. Immediately after giving their hearers Bibles (*CTW*, p. 112), sponsors may also give them personalized copies of the *Hymnal* while the catechist says:
> Receive this book of hymnody and worship.
> Sing with us the praises of the God who saves us;
> and let the prayers and songs in this book
> be on your lips and in your heart.

2. THE HYMNAL IS A WITNESS TO MANY VOICES

One of the things United Methodists believe about the church is that it is catholic, meaning "pertaining to the whole" or "universal," not the name of a denomination. In today's fragmented society, people need to hear the good news that God intends the church to embrace all peoples and communities. *The United Methodist Hymnal* and *Mil Voces* can open up a world of rich diversity revealing the catholicity of the church.

The *Hymnal* contains hymns and other music from the spectrum of voices that make up the choir that is United Methodism today: African American, Asian American, Hispanic, Native American, European American. In addition, the *Hymnal* makes available a range of hymns from the twenty centuries of the life of the Christian church. Thus, the *Hymnal* exposes United Methodists to the diversity and unity of the body of Christ through time.

A creative use of this rich musical testimony to the gospel will perhaps do more to introduce the idea of the catholicity of the church than any lecture. Consider these possibilities:

- Formational group sessions could begin and end with hymns from the diverse traditions represented in the *Hymnal.*
- Hearers could use the lyrics of the hymns as devotional readings to complement their meditations on Scripture.
- Hymns could easily form an important element of the regular worship life of hearers as they meet in small groups.
- Hearers can be shown how to use the indexes of the *Hymnal* (pp. 923-926; MV, pp. 417-426) to enrich their devotional life.
- A diverse selection of hymns (traditional and contemporary) can be used in congregational worship. It not only enriches the worship life of the congregation but also provides rich resources for reflection in formational group sessions.

3. THE HYMNAL IS A DIVERSE LITURGICAL RESOURCE

Expose hearers to the rich catholicity of The United Methodist Church by using the variety of musical and liturgical resources of the different racial-ethnic communities in the church. The new Hispanic United Methodist hymnal, *Mil Voces*, contributes a wealth of musical and liturgical resources to the church. Other resources, such as *Hymns from the Four Winds, Songs of Zion, Voices,* and *Come Sunday: The Liturgy of Zion,* offer the gifts of Native American and African-American Methodist worship traditions. Some of the hymns and prayers from these books appear in *The United Methodist Hymnal,* but those responsible for planning worship specifically for hearers would benefit from the more comprehensive range of music and prayers in these other resources.

- Arrange with the church's worship team to use a variety of racial-ethnic hymns and prayers in congregational worship. Reflect on these worship experiences in formational group sessions.
- Formational group sessions could begin and end with hymns from the racial-ethnic resources.

4. THE HYMNAL IS A SOURCE OF COMMON TEXTS FOR REFLECTION

In United Methodism the texts of the Sunday service (opening prayer, prayers of confession, prayers of the people or pastoral prayer, the Great Thanksgiving, and so forth) have not generally served as sources for reflection on what it means to be a Christian. They serve as something the pastor and/or the liturgist does on Sunday morning; but they are not seen as the property of every Christian.

In contrast to this view, I believe that the words of the Sunday service should be owned by every member of the congregation. This is probably not a typical United Methodist perspective. For many if not most United Methodists, the texts for the Sunday service come neither from the *Hymnal* nor from the *Book of Worship*; they are composed by the pastor for a particular Sunday. Thus, these texts are viewed as the pastor's, not the people's. At best, the prayers are written with pastoral sensitivity and attention to historic patterns of Christian prayer. At worst, they are idiosyncratic, devoid of theological content, and a hindrance to the congregation's expression of praise. They are not owned by the people so much as they are patiently endured.

In contrast, the prayers (and hymns) of the *Hymnal, Mil Voces,* and the *Book of Worship* have the "seal of approval" of the denomination. More than any other set of texts, these can claim to speak for United Methodism in a way others cannot.

These suggestions may seem to fly in the face of the much-treasured Methodist tradition of free prayer. Yet in this era of transdenominationalism, when people from a range of Christian traditions become members of United Methodist congregations, the task of formation requires United Methodists to be able to refer to a common body of liturgical texts so that the church is able to clearly state and teach United Methodist belief and practice.

- In formational group sessions, have hearers reflect on their experiences in worship of the church's common prayers and other texts. Discuss how these experiences may help hearers respond to the threshold questions of the formation stage. If your pastor does not regularly use the liturgical texts and actions found in the *Hymnal*, talk to her or him about using these texts and actions during the formation stage.

5. THE HYMNAL IS A BOOK OF ACTIONS

One of your goals as a catechist is to help people live into what they do and say on Sunday. This is particularly important during the formation stage when hearers test their desire to be baptized and to find life within the church. Participation in public worship and in formational group sessions is crucial for helping hearers respond to God's Word and relate their lives to the gospel.

In considering how you can do this, let's expand our understanding of worship to include not only texts but also actions. In a sense, what we *do* in worship is more fundamental than what we *say*. Through history, the words of Christian worship have varied considerably; the actions they accompany, however, have remained remarkably consistent.

Figure 4
The Actions of Worship
Entrance
Proclamation and Response
Thanksgiving and Communion
Sending Forth

Recognizing that worship is as much action as it is words, the *Hymnal* and *Mil Voces* begin the "General Services," (found in *UMH*, pp. 2-54) not with a full-blown order for the Sunday service (complete with texts) but with a simple order of *actions*: Entrance, Proclamation and Response, Thanksgiving and Communion, and Sending Forth (*UMH*, p. 2).

We should attend to the actions of worship as much as, if not more than, the words that accompany them. Not that the words are unimportant; we need them. But Christian formation will be greatly assisted by a congregation that understands that worship is something *done* as much as it is something *said*. Such a congregation will draw hearers into the great dance of the Sunday service where Christians gather to hear and proclaim the Word of God, to respond to the Word in prayer, to give thanks to God over bread and wine, and to receive the body and blood of Christ—all to serve the world in Christ's name.

If we take the actions of worship seriously, much of our worship will have to change, as will the way we plan it. We will need to attend to how each action of the service can most fully happen.

As you think about how to use the resources of the *Hymnal*, consider these possibilities:

- As your formational group enters a different season of the Christian Year, begin each group session with the prayer for that season from *The United Methodist Hymnal*. (See the list under "Christian Year" on page 937 of the *Hymnal*. The items appearing in italics are prayers for a particular season of the year.)
- If your formational group includes a regular time of worship, use the appropriate order of daily praise and prayer (*UMH*, pp. 876-879).
- To conclude formational group sessions, select from the variety of prayers in *The United Methodist Hymnal*. (See, for example, 69, 329, 456, 481, 493, 495, 531, 570, 607, 639, 705, 894-896.)

WORSHIP AND THE INTENSIVE PREPARATION STAGE

During the weeks of Lent or Advent, candidates preparing for baptism consider these threshold questions: "Do you renounce the spiritual forces of wickedness, and repent of your sin? Do you confess Jesus Christ as Savior and Lord?" (*CTW*, p. 102)

Perhaps the most important thing you can do about worship during the stage of intensive preparation is to help candidates reflect on these questions in light of their upcoming baptisms. Take time during formational group sessions for candidates to process what they have experienced in worship services, including services of initiation.

Consider these possibilities:

- "A Service for Calling Persons to Baptism" (*CTW*, pp. 113-115) powerfully expresses that being called to baptism involves an entire community of people, not just the person to be baptized. Have candidates ponder questions like:
  a. What was going through your mind as you stood in front of the congregation and said that you wanted to be baptized?
  b. Did you feel surrounded by a community of faith? Why or why not?
  c. What does it feel like to have begun this time of intensive preparation for baptism? What are your hopes and fears?

There are no "right" answers to these questions, of course. They are designed to stimulate discussion, which you can guide into a reflection on the Gospel readings for Lent or Advent, readings that stress Jesus' power to save us.

- In formational group sessions, as candidates examine their lives and weigh accepting Christ's call to belong to God's reign, ask candidates to view their congregational worship experiences in light of these questions: "What must change (die) in you in order that Christ's reign of love and justice may flourish in your life? How will you live for Jesus in your daily life?" (CTW, p. 106) These questions could also be adapted for use with listening to the reading of Scripture.

- Consider applying the sign of the cross with oil on the foreheads of the newly-baptized. This action may happen after the candidates have been baptized and have experienced the laying on of hands. These actions symbolize the work of the Holy Spirit in the believer's life. (See UMBOW, p. 91.) The sign of the cross is valuable because the cross stands at the center of our faith. Without it, there would be no good news, no freedom from sin. The sign of the cross reminds Christians powerfully of their baptisms, when they were sealed with the Spirit of God and made part of Christ's living body, the church. Applying the sign of the cross during baptism reminds the newly-baptized of their commitments to renounce the spiritual forces of wickedness, to repent of their sin, and to confess Jesus Christ as Savior and Lord. In other words, the sign of the cross helps baptized believers remember who and whose they are.

WORSHIP AND THE INTEGRATION STAGE

As Come to the Waters makes clear, baptism "must never be seen as arrival or graduation" (p. 108). During the integration stage following baptism, new Christians encounter the threshold questions, "How will you endeavor to follow Jesus Christ under the guidance of the Holy Spirit? What is your sense of calling? What support do you need from other Christians in order to continue as Christ's faithful disciple?" (CTW, p. 103) Reflection on these questions helps the newly-baptized become integrated into the life of the congregation, discern a calling to Christian ministry in daily life, and ascertain the support needed for ongoing faithful discipleship.

The issues of living as part of a sacramental community, of a call to ministry, and of mutual support in discipleship are fundamental to worship.

Meaningful participation in the sacramental community of the church will not happen automatically, especially if your congregation has not spent the time and effort to reflect on the meanings and implications of participation in the sacraments of baptism and the Lord's Supper. New Christians anticipate the public affirmation of their callings to ministry which happens during "A Service for Affirmation of Ministry in Daily Life" (on Pentecost Sunday or Tranfiguration Sunday). In the period leading up to that service, participation in a healthy, dynamic sacramental life (both inside and outside of worship) is essential for formation to take place.

Several suggestions follow about how new Christians may begin to live out of the rhythms of the church's sacramental life, especially as they experience God's continuing grace and call to ministry and witness in daily life.

1. REFLECT ON AND EXPERIENCE THE SACRAMENTS

Formation during the integration stage requires two elements: (a) explicit teaching on the meaning and implications of the sacraments for daily life; and (b) frequent (preferably weekly) celebrations of the Eucharist.

Here are several suggestions about how to incorporate these two elements in worship and in formational group sessions:

Reflect on the meaning of baptism and the Lord's Supper

We are fortunate to have available today a variety of excellent resources on the meaning of the sacraments. For teaching what United Methodists believe about baptism, use the denomination-wide study of baptism, *By Water and the Spirit,* approved by the 1996 General Conference. This study states the church's official position on the theology and practice of baptism. Accompanied by historical, theological, and pastoral commentary written by Gayle C. Felton, it appears in the Christian Initiation series under the title *By Water and the Spirit: Making Connections for Identity and Ministry* (Nashville: Discipleship Resources, 1997).

Two good resources about the sacraments for new Christians are William H. Willimon's *Remember Who You Are: Baptism and the Christian Life* (Nashville: Upper Room Books, 1980) and his *Sunday Dinner: The Lord's Supper and the Christian Life* (Nashville: Upper Room Books, 1981). More detailed historical and theological discussions appear in the two volumes by Laurence Stookey, *Baptism: Christ's Act in the Church* and *Eucharist: Christ's Feast with the Church.* In conjunction with Felton's volume, Stookey's texts would make an excellent resource for catechists and pastors preparing to teach about the sacraments. Another good resource is the Faith and Order convergence text *Baptism, Eucharist and Ministry* (Faith and Order Paper 111, Geneva: WCC Publications, 1982). *BEM,* as this document is called, represents the fruit of more than fifty years of ecumenical reflection on the sacraments by the member churches of the World Council of Churches' Faith and Order Commission. *BEM* should be read in conjunction with the United Methodist bishops' response to *BEM,* which appears in volume two of the series *Churches Respond to BEM* (Geneva: WCC Publications, 1986, pp. 177-199). Finally, in light of the recent General Conference decision to move forward with the Consultation on Church Union covenanting proposal, you may also want to consider using the material on worship, baptism, and the Lord's Supper in *The COCU Consensus: In Quest of a Church of Christ Uniting* (1984, pp. 35-38). A study edition of the *Consensus* is also available, making this important text available for congregational reflection.

It would be easy to turn this time of reflection into a class about sacramental theology. Resist that urge! The goal is to foster the practice of thinking about what the newly-baptized experience in the sacraments, using three kinds of questions:

- What is the meaning of the sacraments for my life and for my calling to ministry?
- What is the meaning of the sacraments for the congregation and for our desire to live together as faithful disciples of Jesus Christ?
- What is the meaning of the sacraments for the church's mission to make disciples of Jesus Christ?

The formational group's reflection on the sacraments should attend to the material elements of the sacraments: bread and wine, water and oil. *Gracious Voices* (pp. 111-126) has much material about the sacraments from Christians through the centuries; it can be very helpful in stimulating reflection and discussion. For the sacraments to have integrity, the Eucharist in your church needs to be celebrated with bread that looks and tastes like bread, and baptism should use ample amounts of water (and oil, if it is used). It is easier, for example, to reflect on the "one loaf" of the Eucharist if a loaf of bread is used at Communion.

At the same time, do not limit the formational group's reflections to the material elements. The *actions* of the sacraments are also central to their power: receiving, offering, breaking, pouring, gathering. Because we use some of these actions in our everyday lives, the newly-baptized will be able to make connections between these actions and what they do in their lives in the world.

Experience the Eucharist frequently

As I have noted, experiencing the sacraments is an important part of the ongoing formation of all Christians. A key to the formative power of the Eucharist (the repeatable part of baptism) is the frequent, at least weekly, experience of it. How can we provide the liturgical space in which weekly participation in the Lord's Supper can take place? There are a number of possibilities.

The best option is for your congregation to celebrate a service of Word and Table (Lord's Supper) at its main Sunday service every week. This setting shows the relationship between the Eucharist as the sacrament of unity and the gathered congregation as the ones to be sent forth in ministry in daily life. It also makes visible on a regular basis the status of all baptized Christians as members of a royal priesthood, offering praise and thanksgiving to God in the Eucharist. Most important, the weekly service of Word and Table will nourish new Christians—indeed, the whole congregation and its ministry— with the Word of God heard and the Word of God made visible. Currently, most United Methodist congregations do not celebrate the Lord's Supper at the main Sunday service each week, although there is an encouraging trend toward that.

If your congregation does not celebrate the Eucharist weekly, there are two things you can do. First, your congregation can make the celebrations of the Lord's Supper as festive as possible, giving special attention to full participation from all members of the congregation. Such celebrations make visible and tangible the central relationship between Sunday as the weekly feast of the resurrection of Jesus and the church's thanksgiving for and *anamnesis* (remembrance, memorial) of Christ in the Eucharist. (See *UMBOW*, pp. 13-40, for suggestions about how to celebrate the service of Word and Table with festivity.) Sunday is the day when Christians should remember, "Christ is risen!" and experience this in the breaking of the bread.

Second, on the Sundays when there is not Word *and* Table at the main service, your congregation could start another Sunday morning service for the newly-baptized, their sponsors, the catechists, and other members of the congregation. Participants can read and proclaim the Word, pray for the church and world, and celebrate the Lord's Supper. However, if there is to be a separate service for the newly-baptized, it is very important that other members be present. Their presence links the celebration with the entire congregation and prevents these services from becoming a separate "baptismal group" within the congregation.

2. PARTICIPATE IN LAY LITURGICAL MINISTRIES

Up to this point in the process of initiation, initiates have not as yet participated in any of the ministries of public worship in which laity take part (such as reading Scripture, leading prayers, acting as the psalmist or usher, serving as a Communion steward or assistant). The integration stage is the time to encourage such participation.

No one should pressure new Christians to sign up for worship ministries. Yet one of the most powerful signs of the priesthood of all believers is the full lay participation in liturgical ministries. There are resources available for training laity to be readers, leaders of prayers, Communion stewards, ushers, and Communion assistants.

Deacons can be particularly helpful in training the newly-baptized for participation in worship services through these ministries. Do not hesitate to ask deacons for help.

3. PRACTICE "THE LITURGY AFTER THE LITURGY"

The most important thing about worship that the newly-baptized can learn in this stage is that all of life is worship—all one does is an offering to God in response to God's love. The times when Christians gather to worship God are special moments in a continuous life of loving service in God's name. But the "work of the people" (which is what the word "liturgy" means) is ultimately to be done in the world, using the gifts God has so graciously given us. In the 1970s, Orthodox theologians, working in ecumenical dialogue, coined the phrase "the liturgy after the liturgy" to describe this reality.[7]

This idea stands at the heart of the post-baptismal period of integration, and during this time you should be particularly attentive to helping the newly-baptized make connections between what they do on Sundays and how they live their lives during the rest of the week. Indeed, one of the threshold questions touches on the need for these connections:

> What is your sense of calling? How will your life be offered as a living sacrifice in the community of Christ's royal priesthood and in the world? How is God calling you to ministry in daily life? Who or what in your world needs the love of God and your active attention? (*CTW*, p. 108)

Coming to see and live out the connections between Sunday worship and daily life is a lifelong endeavor. Therefore, you may wish to gather the newly-baptized and more experienced Christians to reflect on this issue in light of the Word of God. Consider asking questions such as these:

- What does being a reader (or psalmist, assistant in Communion, and so forth) have to do with ministry in the world?
- How do the actions of worship (Entrance, Proclamation and Response, Thanksgiving and Communion, Sending Forth) help us envision our ministry in the world?
- As United Methodists, we believe in the priesthood of all believers. How are we to be priests to the world around us?

RESOURCES

Hymns from the Four Winds: A Collection of Asian American Hymns. Nashville: Abingdon, 1983.

McClain, William B. *Come Sunday: The Liturgy of Zion.* Nashville: Abingdon, 1990.

Mil Voces Para Celebrar: Himnario Metodista. Nashville: United Methodist Publishing House, 1996.

Native American Hymnal and Worship Resource Committee. *Voices: Native American Hymns and Worship Resources.* Nashville: Discipleship Resources, 1992.

Saliers, Don E. *Worship as Theology: Foretaste of Glory Divine.* Nashville: Abingdon, 1994.

Songs of Zion. Nashville: Abingdon, 1981.

White, James F. *Sacraments as God's Self Giving.* Nashville: Abingdon, 1983.

Chapter Four

PRAYER AND THE DISCIPLINED LIFE

"...Lord, teach us to pray...." (Luke 11:1)

What is the goal of prayer and the disciplined life in formation?

To form inquirers, hearers, candidates, and the newly-baptized into people of prayer by creating a space for disciplined prayer in their daily lives.

Prayer nourishes the pilgrimage of conversion as much as the bread of the Word does. To return to our gardening metaphor, prayer is like the air needed by plants to live and to grow. It is also like the light of the sun and the rain that moistens the dry earth. Prayer is essential to the life of believers, and it is as readily available to us as the air we breathe.

At the same time, prayer is not something that comes easily or naturally. The disciples' request to Jesus, "Lord, teach us to pray" (Luke 11:1), indicates that they did not know how to pray. They expected Jesus (like other Jewish teachers of his time) to have his own teaching on the subject. The very fact that he was a teacher meant that he was seen as someone who knew how to pray and how to teach others to pray.

When people become hearers, they enter into the life of the church. Prayer is part of that life; it is the lifeblood of the church. The church serves as a school of prayer for both initiates and experienced Christians. Therefore, the prayer life adopted in the process of initiation will continue through the initiates' lives. Remember, the initiation process is not designed to create "super-Christians" who excel in the disciplines. The process nurtures the seed of the Word planted in people's hearts and helps the seed to establish strong roots. So, when life becomes difficult, faith will not wither and die.

This chapter discusses how initiates begin their training in prayer. In addition, we will mention other disciplines the formational group can consider adopting: journaling, fasting, daily meditation on the Word, and commemoration of the saints. Only the practices of prayer and meditation on the Word are *essential* for all stages of initiation. Journaling can be quite appropriate for all four stages. The same is true for the commemoration of the saints. Fasting more properly belongs to the days of intensive preparation for baptism.

In proposing these practices, I do not intend to impose discipline for discipline's sake. Disciplines are always for the sake of the Christian, not the other way around. Disciplines aim at "preparing the soil" for the conversion of the heart. These disciplines can be valuable aids in the daily battle with all that keeps us from God.

Experienced Christians know, as Christians have known through the centuries, that discipleship is a life-and-death struggle fought daily. In this age of feel-good spirituality and easy solutions, catechists need to teach this wisdom to initiates. To represent the way of the gospel as anything less is to misrepresent it. Such misrepresentation can inevitably lead to disappointment and frustration when the road becomes difficult.

PRAYER AND THE INQUIRY STAGE

If a formational group for inquirers exists, the catechist can decide on the place of prayer in the group. However, if sponsors are the main contacts with whom inquirers explore the questions of faith, the sponsors will determine how to teach about prayer.

Prayer may be the avenue through which some inquirers come to a deeper exploration of the gospel. An answered prayer, the experience of being sustained by the prayers of others through a difficult time, other encounters with prayer and the people who pray—all of these can draw people to explore the Christian faith.

There is no fixed way to talk about Christian prayer to people who may have little or no Christian experience. Individuals are unique, and their experiences must be respected when discussing the threshold questions of this stage.

As you prepare to teach inquirers about prayer, consider this possibility:

- In cooperation with sponsors, explore the role of prayer as inquirers ponder the threshold questions: "What are you seeking? What is happening in your life that prompts your search?" (*CTW*, p. 104) Pray with inquirers, using words that express gratitude for this time of searching and for God's love.

PRAYER AND THE FORMATION STAGE

The busyness of the world rages around us every day. The hurried pace we maintain may be the biggest obstacle to prayer and the most difficult to overcome. We all have many responsibilities; after all, we have important roles to play in our families, in our jobs, and in the church.

How can we pray when finding the time to hear ourselves think seems impossible? This lack of rest, silence, and listening is profoundly corrosive to the heart. Being formed in the way of Christ means learning a new way to live, a way that makes room for silence, reflection, and prayer. Creating that space in one's life means making hard choices. It involves questioning, in light of the gospel, the commitments we have made.

During the formation stage, hearers assess their desire to be a Christian and to live as a Christian disciple. The threshold questions they face are: "Do you desire to be baptized? Do you desire life with the church?" (*CTW*, p. 102) As they explore the basic patterns of Christian living, hearers in formational groups should be encouraged to connect faith with daily life, asking, "[How is] God active [in the settings] of family, leisure, work, community, church and national or global concerns?" (*CTW*, p. 106) In seeking to make these connections, prayer plays a crucial role.

To help hearers discover God's gracious presence in the various settings of their daily lives, it is important that they find time to pray each day, even briefly. Developing this discipline in hearers is also the chief challenge catechists face during the formation stage. To be sure, hearers need information about prayer, but the best way to learn about prayer is to *pray*.

The formation stage is a time for practice, practice, practice. Hearers will learn that Christians never stop practicing. Perhaps the most important thing catechists can do during this stage is to help establish and nurture the practice of prayer in each hearer.

What do hearers need to know about prayer? In ancient Christianity, catechumens learned the Lord's Prayer and the traditions of interpreting that prayer. They were instructed to pray three times a day. They were also supported by the widespread practice of praying at set times each day, with other Christians if they happened to be present. Finally, once they had been baptized, they were supported by the community's weekly celebration of the Eucharist. Thus, they were supported in the individual and corporate dimensions of their prayer life.

Christians today can learn something from these early practices, particularly the idea that prayer is never a purely individual act. Prayer always takes place in the context of the body of Christ, even when a person prays alone. Christians can also relearn the wisdom of Christian experience that stresses the absolute necessity of a reliance on God through prayer in daily life.

Relying on God may be one of the most difficult lessons for Christians in North American society to learn. We like to think that we are self-sufficient. When we have this attitude, our first serious encounter with temptation (or the sense of spiritual listlessness) will deal a severe blow, leaving us feeling guilty and inadequate: "If only I had tried harder (had been a better person, and so forth)...." In turn, these feelings sometimes prevent us from resuming our walk in faith.

To help hearers develop a lifestyle of disciplined prayer, consider these possibilities:

1. Show Hearers a Simple Way to Pray Daily

Encourage hearers to pray daily, whether they feel like it or not. The temptation to forego prayer when we feel spiritually "dry" affects even the most experienced Christian. But it is at times such as these that regular prayer is needed most.

What constitutes a "simple" practice of prayer? Catechists need to judge how each hearer could best be served by a regular prayer life in conjunction with any of the other disciplines. There is no one-size-fits-all system of prayer. Discerning the type of prayer that fits each hearer takes time, patience, and trust in the guidance of the Spirit.

When it comes to learning how to pray, more is not better. A spiritual life is not about doing a lot of different things. The life of discipleship is about loving and trusting God in all of the circumstances of our lives, not about learning elaborate disciplines.

The most important elements of an initial prayer practice are the reading and meditation on God's Word and the cultivation of the habit of putting oneself in God's presence throughout the day.[8]

Hearers could begin by taking five or ten minutes at the start of the day to read the week's Gospel lesson, listening for a phrase or sentence that stands out. They should keep this passage in mind throughout the day. Although the time demand may seem small, some hearers may at first have difficulty adapting to the structured schedule. Suggest that these hearers take some time, however short or long, at the beginning of the day to read the Gospel, and prayerfully see what happens.

Emphasize that the important thing in prayer life is cultivating the "practice of the presence of God" (to use Brother Lawrence's phrase). An excellent way to practice God's presence is to use a form of the Jesus Prayer made famous by *The Way of a Pilgrim*. Ask each hearer to choose a word or phrase connected to the Christian faith that has meaning for her or him. It could be the name "Jesus" or perhaps a phrase taken from the Psalms. The traditional phrase is: "Lord Jesus Christ, Son of God, have mercy on me, a sinner." Then, ask hearers to repeat the word or phrase throughout the day, putting themselves in God's presence as they say it.

The wonderful thing about this practice is that it can be done anywhere, particularly at times when life gets stressful. Over time, the practice takes root and opens people to see God's work in the world. It sensitizes them to the many occasions in daily life when God calls them to pray for others and to extend God's love.

It is important that every hearer adopts a practice of daily prayer and sticks to it. Learning how to pray is similar to getting in shape physically. You have to exercise every day to see results.

2. Encourage Hearers to Pray the Lord's Prayer Daily

The foundation of all Christian prayer is the Lord's Prayer. If there is a set prayer hearers should pray daily, this is it. *The United Methodist Hymnal* (894) contains an ecumenical version of this jewel.

The earliest Christian treatises on prayer (written by the third-century theologians Origen and Tertullian) are interpretations of the Lord's Prayer. Through the centuries the Lord's Prayer has remained a favorite text for commentators, and much information about the prayer is available.

Gracious Voices (pp. 81-110) contains a rich selection of the church's accumulated experience with the Lord's Prayer. Use these selections in formational group sessions to help hearers reflect on the meaning of the Lord's Prayer for their daily lives as they make the journey toward baptism.

3. Encourage the Practice of Daily Common Prayer

Christians of the first century derived from Judaism the custom of praying together at fixed times of the day: morning, noon, evening, and night. Early Christian writings admonished laypeople to pray as often as seven times a day. After the legalization of Christianity in the fourth century, many congregations held a public service of prayer and praise in the morning and evening, while the growing monastic movements of the fourth century took over the older hours of prayer intended for all Christians.

Catechists have at their disposal a wealth of daily prayer resources. The United Methodist services of morning prayer and praise and evening prayer and praise (*UMH*, pp. 876-879) are the first in any Methodist hymnal, and it represents a twentieth-century reclamation of the fourth-century congregational liturgies of daily prayer (known as the "cathedral office"). The content of both services obviously focuses on praise and prayer, with the possibility of including meditation and readings from Scripture. Where appropriate, catechists could easily use these liturgies in formational group sessions.

Other resources exist for formational groups who want to pray together. The *Book of Common Worship* of the Presbyterian Church (USA) contains many materials for daily prayer, including the Psalter. The *Book of Common Prayer, 1979* (pp. 36-146) of The Episcopal Church includes not only versions of the traditional Anglican services of morning prayer and evening prayer but also forms for noonday prayer, prayer at night (compline), and daily devotions for individuals and families, based on the structure of the daily offices. Job and Shawchuck's *A Guide to Prayer* provides readers with a daily structure of reading, meditation, and prayer that can be used by individuals or groups. Lastly, *The Upper Room Worshipbook: Music and Liturgies for Spiritual Formation* (112-117) contains services for daily prayer, plus musical resources.

How realistic is it to expect a group that is made up of busy people to find the time to gather regularly for daily prayer? It is probably not very realistic at all. We need to remember that even in the fourth century, "star" preachers such as John Chrysostom had difficulty getting their congregation members to pray daily! However, when the formational group does meet, it will pray according to a common pattern.

Daily common prayer involves the life of the congregation as a whole. Many congregations do not have a daily cycle of morning and evening prayer. It may not be prudent for catechists to insist that the congregation begin such a cycle. However, catechists may certainly suggest that the congregation learn to take advantage of the times when it gathers to celebrate short liturgies of reading, psalmody, intercessory prayer, and thanksgiving. If a congregation can come to see that prayer and the act of gathering naturally belong together, it may be possible that daily morning and evening prayer cycles can become a reality. If this were to happen, it would be a boon to the process of initiation.

In lieu of meeting together for prayer, a formational group could covenant to pray each day at a specified time, using a designated form of prayer. (The individual devotions in the *Book of Common Prayer, 1979* of The Episcopal Church [pp. 136-140] provide a brief prayer service for morning, noon, early evening, and at the close of the day). Whatever form is used, the aim of such a prayer is to provide spiritual support for the members of the group, intercessory prayer for the needs of the world, and an opportunity to confess sin and thank God for God's blessings. Remind hearers that we never truly pray alone. We pray as members of the body of Christ and as people in whom the Spirit of God dwells. The Spirit, in turn, prays for us.

As you consider the suggestions in these paragraphs, be sure to prompt hearers to reflect on the many ways they can live prayerfully; also, with the hearers, reflect on their experiences of God in prayer.

4. ENCOURAGE HEARERS TO USE THE PSALMS IN DAILY PRAYER

The monastic communities of the fourth century introduced the practice of reciting the entire Psalter every week. For the monks of Egypt, Palestine, and Cappadocia, reciting the Book of Psalms in one week (or even in one day) was a spiritual discipline aimed at the perfection of the individual monk. As a result, the course reading of the Psalms entered daily prayer in western and eastern Christianity. The old cathedral office discussed earlier also included psalmody, but only those deemed appropriate to the time of day (that is, morning and evening).

Today, many Christians are rediscovering the great value of the Psalms as prayer texts that embrace the range of human emotions and experiences. The early church understood the Psalms in light of Christ, recognizing both references to Christ and Christ's work, as well as to Christ speaking. Today, we can view the Psalms as witnesses to Israel's life with God, proclamations of the God of Israel who is faithful and full of loving kindness, and as texts Jesus knew and cherished. Christians can also read the Psalms as a way of celebrating their faith in the Risen Christ.

There are several good translations of the Psalms available today. *The United Methodist Hymnal* (pp. 736-862) contains a selection of Psalms for singing, along with at least one antiphon (a type of response) per psalm. Note that not all of the Psalms appointed in the Revised Common Lectionary appear in the *Hymnal*; moreover, of the two Psalms that appear almost universally through the centuries in morning and evening prayer (Psalm 63 and Psalm 141), only the former is included in the *Hymnal.* A striking translation of the psalms was prepared recently by the International Commission on English in the Liturgy (ICEL), a Roman Catholic body responsible for translations of liturgical texts for the use of English-speaking Roman Catholics. This translation seeks to preserve some of the tone and even the sentence structure of the Hebrew text. It would make a fine translation to read aloud or use for meditation.

Where can a list of psalms for daily prayer be found? Three sources are particularly helpful. First, a complete Psalter divided into morning and evening readings for each month of the year is included in the 1979 *Book of Common Prayer* (pp. 585-808). Also included in this resource is a daily prayer lectionary that focuses on a psalm (or psalms) for each day as it follows the liturgical year. Second, a web site called Universalis (**http://www.universalis.com**) provides the daily psalms according to the Liturgy of the Hours of the Roman Catholic Church. This site also links with other daily prayer resources on the World Wide Web. Third, the weekly psalm appointed in the Revised Common Lectionary could easily be prayed each day of the following week.

Finally, to help hearers make the Psalms a part of their prayer, your congregation may decide to give each hearer a copy of the Book of Psalms. There are several translations available in inexpensive pocket editions. Among the many options, the Psalter produced by the International Commission on English in the Liturgy (ICEL) stands out because of its inclusive language and its beautiful printed form. Another good option is the Psalter of the *Book of Common Prayer.*

5. ENCOURAGE HEARERS TO START A JOURNAL

Keeping a daily journal of thoughts, observations, insights, and questions is a good way for hearers to develop a greater self-awareness and a greater sense of the work God is doing in their lives.

Initiates should begin keeping a journal during the formation stage and continue the practice throughout the process of initiation.

There are many approaches to journaling. In the context of the journey toward baptism, a journal should focus on the threshold questions appropriate to each stage of the process of initiation. Initiates may reflect each day on the week's lectionary readings and the threshold questions.

In addition to the threshold questions, initiates may also ponder these three questions at any stage of the initiation process:
- Where do I see God working in my daily life?
- Where do I hear God calling me to greater faithfulness?
- What questions about being a faithful disciple does my experience raise?

The purpose of writing down one's thoughts, feelings, questions, and observations at the end of each day is to help develop the discipline of attentive watchfulness.

As with any discipline, journaling can be abused. For example, giving undue attention to every small action or deed may border on self absorption and defeat the purpose of journaling, which is to discover where God's grace and forgiveness are working in our lives. If keeping a journal leads to constant guilt or preoccupation with sinful actions, these are signs that the initiate needs guidance from the pastor about the role of grace and forgiveness in Christian life. Richard Foster's *Celebration of Discipline* discusses journaling in some detail, and it should be read by anyone interested in beginning a journal.

6. Encourage Hearers to Commemorate the Saints

The well-known Wesley hymn "Come, Let Us Join Our Friends Above" says,
> One family we dwell in him,
> one church above, beneath,
> though now divided by the stream,
> the narrow stream of death. (*UMH*, No. 709)

Yet, for most of their history, American Methodists have not formally celebrated the saints by a sanctoral (a calendar of saints' days). When he abridged the 1662 *Book of Common Prayer* of the Church of England for the soon-to-be-formed Methodist Episcopal Church, John Wesley eliminated the saints' days because he thought they had lost their usefulness for Christians of his time.

The day may have come again when the commemoration of saints can serve a valuable purpose. Christian formation requires role models or mentors; we need to see and learn how to be a Christian. The United Methodist Church exists in a society that cannot provide such role models; therefore, the church must look once again to the Christians of the past and present who made and make visible the redeeming, sanctifying love of God in Christ. Sponsors and catechists can become mentors for hearers while the saints can provide another type of role model.

United Methodists now have an unofficial sanctoral, *For All the Saints: A Calendar of Commemorations for United Methodists,* edited by Clifton Guthrie.[9] It draws upon the Methodist, Evangelical, and United Brethren traditions, and also includes people commemorated by other traditions. The book includes a brief biography of each person profiled and prayers to use when commemorating the saints.

Catechists can use *For All the Saints* in the formation process in a variety of ways. Consider these possibilities:

- In formational group sessions:
  a. When reading a selection from *Gracious Voices* that was written or said by a person commemorated in *For All the Saints*, read the person's biography. (Hearers and sponsors may also do this outside group sessions.)
  b. If a group meets on a day commemorating a particular person, begin the session by reading the biography from *For All the Saints* and by offering a prayer of thanksgiving for the person. Take time to discuss the person's example and how we can emulate it today.
  c. Use *For All the* Saints as a way to lead the group in a discussion of the "communion of saints" and what holiness means.

    d. Ask hearers to choose a patron saint from *For All the Saints*. Encourage them to incorporate the examples set by those saints into their reflection on the meaning of the gospel for their lives.

    e. Ask hearers to name holy people in their lives—people they would like to remember in prayer and celebration.

- In other settings:

Print the commemorations occurring in the upcoming week in the Sunday bulletin. Note these commemorations in the congregation's announcement time. These actions could help the entire membership appreciate the examples of holy women and men through history and provide a way for the congregation to contribute to the formation of hearers.

PRAYER AND THE INTENSIVE PREPARATION STAGE

The intensive preparation stage comprises the weeks of Lent (or Advent and Christmas) and culminates in the service of Holy Baptism at the Easter Vigil (or Baptism of the Lord). During this crucial period candidates focus on the questions to be asked at baptism: "Do you renounce the spiritual forces of wickedness, and repent of your sin? Do you confess Jesus Christ as Savior and Lord?" To answer these questions with integrity, candidates engage in an "[e]xamination of the heart (self-searching and repentance) and enlightenment" (*CTW*, p. 102).

The intensive preparation stage calls for candidates to continue practicing the disciplined prayer life they began during the formation stage, including keeping a daily journal. However, the increasing focus on repentance and self-examination makes this stage ideal for introducing additional spiritual disciplines, rites, and practices, such as fasting and the examination of conscience.

As you lead candidates through the intensive preparation toward baptism, consider these possibilities for formation:

1. OFFER OPPORTUNITIES FOR SPECIAL PRAYER

Come to the Waters (p. 107) suggests the provision of opportunities for prayer and reflection focusing specifically on Jesus' passion and death. Such opportunities may take the form of a retreat, or a vigil at the church. Candidates can examine their commitments to follow Christ's way as they ponder questions such as, "What desires and affections need realignment for you to follow Christ with your whole heart?" (*CTW*, p. 107) Catechists may need to consult with the pastor and the initiation leadership team to determine how these prayer opportunities can be offered.

2. INTRODUCE CANDIDATES TO THE PRACTICE OF FASTING

Come to the Waters (p. 107) recommends the practice of fasting during the intensive preparation stage to help candidates prepare spiritually and emotionally for baptism. Since the practice may be alien to many candidates, it is very important that catechists understand the meaning and rationale for fasting and that they introduce it with care and sensitivity.

In a North American society driven by overconsumption, fasting may seem the most wholesome of all spiritual disciplines. Yet, like any spiritual discipline, it can be misused.

Christians can take part in fasting for its own sake, forgetting that the practice exists for the sake of the heart and its conversion. In no way should catechists impose fasting on candidates for baptism. Instead, exercise discernment and common sense when you recommend the practice.

If you and your pastor agree that fasting is appropriate for your candidates, be sure to stress the following points:

(1) Fasting affirms the goodness of the body and the goodness of the created world. We fast not to punish but to recognize that our bodies and our appetites have as much to do with our spirituality as our hearts.

(2) Fasting involves more than abstaining from food. It also involves abstention from anything that distracts the heart from God. Thus, abstention from food could also be coupled with abstention from television or unloving attitudes, words, and actions.

(3) In a society that practices overconsumption, there is a special ethical dimension to fasting. Catechists may encourage candidates to donate to the hungry the money they would have spent on food. Encourage candidates to think about how their daily lives can be simplified to reduce the unnecessary consumption of the earth's resources.

(4) Fasting is accompanied by prayer. Fasting creates space in our lives for the heart to turn to God in prayer, adoration, and thanksgiving.

(5) Fasting is never an end in and of itself.

In formational group sessions, consider exploring the following possibilities:

• Discuss how candidates may adopt the discipline of fasting one day a week during the weeks of Lent. Allow time in subsequent group sessions to reflect on the experiences of fasting.

• Discuss how the practice of fasting may help candidates prepare emotionally and spiritually for their baptisms. Be sure to relate the discussion to the threshold questions for the intensive preparation stage. In addition, ask how fasting has or has not changed candidates' experiences and understandings of ministry in daily life.

3. Offer Opportunities for the Examination of Conscience

On the third, fourth, and fifth Sundays of Lent (or on the third and fourth Sundays of Advent and the first Sunday after Christmas), candidates may participate in the rite of "Examination of Conscience" (*CTW*, pp. 117-119; see also pp. 77-79 and p. 107 for background material).

The examination of conscience focuses on candidates' preparation for baptism. Prayers are offered for the removal of any habits, attitudes, perceptions, and loyalties that bind candidates in spirit or will. The congregation blesses candidates and prays that Christ may continue to free them from hindrances that keep them from following Christ in the love of God and neighbor. The congregation "prays on candidates' behalf for the grace to say *no* to sin and evil in order to be free to say *yes* to Jesus Christ in daily life" (*CTW*, p. 118); it trusts God's Spirit to do the work of conversion in candidates' (and the congregation's) lives. The examination of conscience is important because it makes clear that all Christians need the liberating power of Christ throughout their lives.

Make certain that candidates understand that this rite is not an opportunity for manipulation or probing. Instead, "[a]s prayer, examinations of conscience are settings in which candidates are supported in their encounters with Jesus" (*CTW*, p. 118); these encounters prepare candidates for baptism and a life of faithful discipleship.

Confer with your pastor and the initiation leadership team about your role as a catechist in this rite. You may be asked to lead or to play another active role in the service.

4. HAND ON THE PRAYER OF THE CHURCH

On the fifth Sunday in Lent (or the Sunday after Christmas or another appropriate Lord's Day), the congregation "gives" the Lord's Prayer to candidates in a rite called "Handing on the Prayer of the Church" (*CTW*, p. 117). Candidates were introduced to this prayer during the formation stage, and many may know the prayer by heart. However, it is important that candidates listen prayerfully as the Christian community hands on the Lord's Prayer in the midst of the Sunday service. This act reflects the handing on of the gospel.

In a sense, the prayer does not belong to the candidates until it has been given to them by the community who owns it; the Lord's Prayer is, after all, the church's prayer. It only makes sense within the context of the body of Christ. Remember, the prayer begins: "*Our* Father" not "*My* Father."

Come to the Waters (p. 117) suggests that each candidate receive a printed copy of the Lord's Prayer during the service to represent a tangible sign of the giftgiving.

- It would be most meaningful if the copies of the Lord's Prayer were crafted (handwritten or illustrated) by members. This would require advance preparation.
- Discuss with your pastor and the leadership initiation team the catechist's role during this service. Catechists need to be actively involved.

PRAYER AND THE INTEGRATION STAGE

The integration stage encompasses the Great Fifty Days and culminates in "A Service for Affirmation of Ministry in Daily Life" on Pentecost Sunday (*CTW*, pp. 120-121). (For candidates baptized on the Sunday of the Baptism of the Lord, the integration stage comprises the remaining weeks after the Baptism of the Lord; the service for affirmation of ministry in daily life takes place on Transfiguration Sunday.)

During the integration stage, the newly-baptized prayerfully seek to discern their God-given call to ministry in the church and in the world. The newly-baptized should continue the prayer life and spiritual disciplines they began in the formation stage. Their prayers will focus on the threshold questions: "How will you endeavor to follow Jesus Christ under the guidance of the Holy Spirit? What is your sense of calling? What support do you need from other Christians in order to continue as Christ's faithful disciple?" (*CTW*, p. 103)

As you lead formational group sessions, consider these possibilities for formation:
- In addition to the threshold questions, ask the newly-baptized Christians to reflect on these questions:
(1) How does prayer relate to ministry in daily life? How does it support that ministry?
(2) How can prayer help me know God's call to ministry for my life?
(3) How do I sustain a prayer life in the midst of the hectic, busy world?
(4) What support do I need from others to continue in prayer?

- Encourage group members to focus on the threshold questions and the previous supplemental questions as they keep their journals. Participants who are willing to share their journal reflections with the group can take the time to do so.
- As a group, consider forming small groups at the conclusion of the initiation process. Group sessions support new Christians in their efforts to sustain an active prayer life and to continue the spiritual disciplines necessary "for living out the cost and the joy of discipleship" (*CTW*, p. 108).

RESOURCES

Bondi, Roberta C. *To Love as God Loves: Conversations with the Early Church.* Minneapolis: Fortress Press, 1987.

————. *To Pray and to Love: Conversations on Prayer with the Early Church.* Minneapolis: Fortress Press, 1991.

————. *In Ordinary Time: Healing the Wounds of the Heart.* Nashville: Abingdon, 1996.

————. *Memories of God: Theological Reflection on a Life.* Nashville: Abingdon, 1995.

Broyles, Anne. *Journaling: A Spirit Journey.* Nashville: Upper Room Books, 1988.

Carden, John, compiler. *A World at Prayer: The New Ecumenical Prayer Cycle.* Mystic: Twenty-Third Publications, 1990.

Eslinger, Elise S., ed. *The Upper Room Worshipbook: Music and Liturgies for Spiritual Formation.* Nashville: Upper Room Books, 1985.

Foster, Richard. *The Celebration of Discipline: The Path to Spiritual Growth.* San Francisco: Harper San Francisco, 1988.

Guthrie, Clifton F., ed. *For All the Saints: A Calendar of Commemorations for United Methodists.* Akron, Ohio: Order of Saint Luke Publications, 1995.

Harris, Maria. *Proclaim Jubilee! A Spirituality for the Twenty-First Century.* Louisville, Kentucky: Westminster John Knox Press, 1996.

International Commission on English in the Liturgy. *The Psalter.* Chicago: Liturgy Training Publications, 1995.

Jones, Alan W. *Soul Making: The Desert Way of Spirituality.* San Francisco: Harper San Francisco, 1989.

Maas, Robin, and Gabriel O' Donnell, eds. *Spiritual Traditions for the Contemporary Church.* Nashville: Abingdon, 1993.

Pennington, M. Basil. *Centering Prayer: Renewing an Ancient Christian Prayer Form.* New York: Doubleday & Co., 1982.

Thurian, Max. *Modern Man and Spiritual Life.* New York: Association Press, 1963.

Washington, James Melvin, ed. *Conversations with God: Two Centuries of Prayers by African Americans.* New York: Harper Perennial Library, 1995.

Weavings: A Journal of the Christian Spiritual Life. Nashville: The Upper Room. This award-winning publication regularly contains articles, stories, and poems on topics pertaining to Christian formation, written by leading figures in contemporary spirituality. A subscription to *Weavings* would be an excellent investment for any congregation undertaking Christian initiation.

Willimon, William H., and Stanley Hauerwas, with Scott C. Saye. *Lord, Teach Us: The Lord's Prayer and Christian Life.* Nashville: Abingdon, 1996.

Chapter Five

MINISTRY IN DAILY LIFE

Sow for yourselves righteousness; reap steadfast love;
break up your fallow ground; for it is time to seek the
LORD, that he may come and rain righteousness upon
you. (Hosea 10:12)

And the king will answer them, "Truly I tell you, just as
you did it to one of the least of these who are members
of my family, you did it to me." (Matthew 25:40)

What is the goal of ministry in daily life in formation?

*To involve initiates in acts of ministry in daily life that form patterns of faithful
Christian discipleship.*

Bear fruit. This is a central theme of the Good News. God calls us not only
to grow but to grow in order to bear fruit. We know that a plant is healthy
and has come to maturity when it produces sound fruit. Likewise, the Word
that God plants in our hearts is intended to grow, producing a rich harvest.
The harvest is love: tangible, visible love, which expresses itself in ministry in daily life.

It is significant that one of the earliest witnesses of Christian initiation, the church
order called the *Apostolic Tradition*, asks not if those who had undergone the rigorous
three-year preparation for baptism had learned correct Christian theology, but if they
had begun to bear the fruits of repentance: living with integrity, visiting the sick, doing
good works (*Apostolic Tradition*, 20). To be sure, the catechumens were taught the .
beliefs of the church, probably through the interpretation of Scripture by a lay or clergy
teacher. As important as that teaching was, though, it is striking that the question of
admittance to final preparation for baptism (during the time that evolved into our season of Lent) ultimately revolved around how a catechumen *lived*. They were to *show*
the fruits of repentance.

As with all that happens in the pilgrimage of Christian initiation, ministry in daily
life has to be seen in the context of God's work of transforming the heart. Conversion
involves deeds as well as words. The Gospels make clear that when Jesus called people, he elicited actions that sprang from their encounter with the Reign of God: paying

back those who had been cheated, telling others about Jesus, going and doing as Jesus had done. In other words, they lived out the Reign of God.

MINISTRY IN DAILY LIFE AND CHRISTIAN FORMATION

Come to the Waters says this about the role of service during formation:

> Leaders should seek to engage those on the journey in the congregation's ministries with the poor and suffering and to reflect with them on the experience of encountering human need in the context of hearing the Word of God. Sponsors and the catechist will seek to bring this dimension of the journey into dialogue with the other elements of Christian initiation: Scripture, prayer, and worship (p. 67).

This dialogue between ministry and Scripture, prayer, and worship needs to be happening in the congregation itself, or it will be difficult to sustain the formative role of ministry in the world for initiates. To engage in this dialogue involves a shift in our thinking about ministry in the world, from viewing it as one activity among many in which the church engages (i.e., part of its "program") to understanding it as a fundamental way of being the church.

In this shift, ministry in the world is considered an act of service, a part of becoming a community of servants. As many writers have noted, Christians use the word "service" to describe both the act of attending to others and the act of worship in which Christians take part on Sundays and at other times. We worship the One who came as one who serves (Luke 22:24-27). Paul exhorted the Roman Christians: "I appeal to you therefore, brothers and sisters, by the mercies of God, to present your bodies as a living sacrifice, holy and acceptable to God, which is your spiritual worship" (Romans 12:1). As people graciously accepted by God and made living members of Christ's body, God calls us to follow the example of Christ's self-offering service. Thus, service is more than something we do, it is who we are.

This kind of ministry in the world is as much an attitude as it is an action. It is a welcoming, embracing stance toward society's marginalized and oppressed. It is a basic orientation toward justice, a way of life that makes visible the servanthood of Christ. This dimension of ministry in daily life saves service from becoming a mere requirement for church membership, an element on a list of things candidates must do before they can be baptized.

Someone may raise the issue of faith versus works: "Are charitable acts just a form of works-righteousness? Through them, aren't we trying to earn God's love?" These are questions John Wesley had to face during his ministry. Remember, the name "Methodist" was used to mock Wesley and his followers for their diligence in doing good works! So why is ministry in daily life not a form of earning salvation? It is because we recognize that all we do is a fruit of God's grace. We cannot earn anything from God because the very ability to do ministry in daily life is a gift from God. Ministry as I am defining it here is a response to God's gracious love in Christ. We do not minister to others to earn God's love; rather, we minister to express God's love for us and for the world. The converted heart will make room for service.

We do ministry in the world because we see that there is tremendous need: hunger, poverty, injustice. We believe that God works in the world. Because God works, we are expected to work also. Each congregation will have to uncover the local community's needs. At the same time, there are basic needs that do not and will not change. Jesus' parable of the Final Judgment sums up these needs:

> ...for I was hungry and you gave me food, I was thirsty and you gave me something to drink, I was a stranger and you welcomed me, I was naked and you gave me clothing, I was sick and you took care of me, I was in prison and you visited me (Matthew 25:35-36).

This parable has guided Christians throughout the centuries as they have striven to serve God in the world. Note the reason that Jesus gives for such service: because it is ultimately service given to him. This is a profound vision, dulled, perhaps, by our over-familiarity with the parable. We do ministry in the world because Christ is in those who are in need. Thus, ministry in the world is not simply about duty; it is a part of a Christian spirituality, a Christian vision of the world.

We respond to those needs because we are members of Christ, who is God's compassion among us. In other words, discipleship embodies the ministering love of God as demonstrated by Christ. Therefore, there are as many ministries in daily life as there are needs in the world.

However, there is something to be said for a common ministry of service in which people preparing for baptism or renewal participate. A common ministry provides a common source of experience for reflection. A common ministry needs to fulfill two criteria: (1) the ministry has to do with meeting the basic human needs (food, shelter, clothing, social support) of the poor and marginalized; and (2) the ministry involves regular interaction with the recipients of the ministry. These criteria assure that the common ministry remains rooted in basic human need and that the ministry is *with*, not *to*, the poor and marginalized.

MINISTRY IN DAILY LIFE AND THE SUNDAY SERVICE

One of your tasks as a catechist is to help candidates make the connections between ministry in the world and worship. A good point of entry for your discussion of the relationship between worship and service is the fact I noted earlier: that in English the word "service" can mean both the giving of oneself on behalf of others and the act of worship (as in "the Sunday service"). The word "liturgy" comes from the Greek word *leitourgia,* which was used by the ancient Greeks for an act of public service. Hebrews uses the word to refer to Christ's high priesthood (Hebrews 8:6); Paul uses the term to refer to sacrificial service in the context of his hymn of praise for Christ who took on the form of a servant (Phillipians 2:17).

Ancient Christians added to these meanings of *leitourgia,* so that their language of serving came to be multi-leveled: the service of Christ in his saving work, the offering of service in response to God's love, the offering of the sacrifice of praise and thanksgiving in the Eucharist. Today in the Eucharist, United Methodists pray that the Holy Spirit will come upon the bread and wine and the people, that they might be "one in ministry (i.e., service) to all the world, until Christ comes in final victory and we feast at his heavenly banquet" (*UMH,* p. 10).[10]

Catechists need to understand that ministry in daily life is not a compartment of discipleship but a way of life; catechists need to help sponsors and initiates recognize this fact. Disciples are servants twenty-four hours a day, seven days a week. Conversion means learning to be attentive to the prompting of Christ's love and care in all things. Resources in the Christian Initiation series use the phrase "ministry in daily life" to stress attentiveness to the needs of others in all circumstances. Unfortunately, for too long the church has taken the view that ministry means involving people in church-sponsored "activities" or "ministries"; this view ignores the fact that Christ has *already* placed the members of his Body in daily settings where ministry is needed.

Catechists are charged with helping those being formed as disciples to discover and obey—right where they are!—the One who calls them to follow. Ministering in the various settings of one's daily life does not make communal forms of ministry unnecessary or inappropriate; indeed, they are both important and needful. However, catechists, together with the initiation leadership team, need to invite the whole congregation—including initiates—to discern what is needed and what God is doing in the many settings of daily life. (See *CTW*, pp. 64-66, for a fuller exploration of these issues.)

Let's turn now to a closer look at the place of ministry in daily life at the inquiry, formation, intensive preparation, and integration stages.

MINISTRY IN DAILY LIFE AND THE INQUIRY STAGE

It is appropriate for the catechist to talk with inquirers about ministry in daily life because the purpose of that ministry is to help inquirers make connections between what is going on in their daily lives and where and how God is at work in the midst of that struggle. In this way, inquirers will be able to deliberate fully the threshold questions of the inquiry stage: "What are you seeking? What is happening in your life that prompts your search?" (*CTW*, p. 104)

In formational group meetings (or in cooperation with sponsors and the pastor, if no formational group exists at this stage), use the issues listed in *Come to the Waters* (pp. 64-65)—family, work, leisure, community, public issues, and faith community—to help inquirers begin "to link discipleship and faith in Christ with the relationships and places in their everyday world" (*CTW*, p. 65).

MINISTRY IN DAILY LIFE AND THE FORMATION STAGE

Because "ministry in daily life" implies that ministry will likely occur apart from the Sunday morning service, sponsors will be a very important part of the hearers' experience at this stage. Here are some ways in which you and the sponsors can work together:

- Before formational groups meet, get together with sponsors to discuss the ministries of your congregation. Plan how to link hearers and their sponsors with specific ministries.
- During the course of the formation period, an entire group session should focus on the experiences of ministry in the world. Make sure that sponsors attend these sessions, and encourage them to add their insights and questions to the discussion.
- Commit a formational group session to a reflection on the Social Principles of The United Methodist Church. (See *The Book of Discipline—1996*, pp. 84-106.)
- In formational group sessions, regularly invite reflection on (1) intentional acts of service to the poor and suffering (see *CTW*, pp. 66-67); and (2) relationships in the settings of daily life, such as the home, the workplace, the community, the world, and the church (see *CTW*, pp. 64-66).
- Talk with your pastor and the sponsors about finding ways to include the hearers in the congregation's ministries of feeding the hungry and providing clothing, money, and assistance to people who are destitute. If your congregation does not have such ministries, then you should help establish a food pantry or a regular

meal program in your church, or become a part of already-established ministries in the community. The point of such ministry is not busywork. To labor in these acts of love is to make God's sustaining, transforming presence evident in the world. Or, to put it another way, God uses and empowers these acts as visible, tangible signs of God's love and presence in the world.

MINISTRY IN DAILY LIFE AND THE INTENSIVE PREPARATION STAGE

Just as formation in prayer, the study of Scripture, and worship intensify during this period, the candidates' reflection on their ministry in the world also intensifies. During the intensive preparation stage, the candidates should reflect in their journals and in formational group sessions on their ministry in the world in light of the questions about their readiness to be baptized into Christ.

Candidates continue to participate in the ministries they joined at the beginning of the formation stage. While the work or service does not change, the questions the candidates ask do change. As we said a moment ago, the issues the candidates entertain at this stage have to do with the momentous decision of becoming a member of the body of Christ and the resulting assumption of the values and practices of that community.

The lens through which candidates view these questions are, typically, the Lenten Gospel readings. It would be good to ask candidates to reflect during the week on their ministries in daily life using these (or similar) questions:

- Becoming a member of the church means taking on the daily sacrifice of self, which obstructs a relationship with God, and a daily resurrection into the life of God in Christ. Where in my ministry in daily life do I hear God calling me to leave behind the old and turn toward life in Christ?
- How do the people with whom I minister in daily life minister to me? What is God saying to me?

MINISTRY IN DAILY LIFE AND THE INTEGRATION STAGE

Entering the community of the church means integrating the church's ethos of ministry in the world into everyday life. This will probably be the most difficult stage of all because it requires that the newly-baptized make basic choices about how they will live their lives in Christ's name. During earlier stages of Christian initiation, ministry in daily life may have been for most initiates an "added extra," one part of the process of formation. Now, after baptism, ministry is to become part of the normal fabric of daily life; now is the time when the "rubber meets the road."

Of course, it is easy to talk about integrating ministry in daily living; it is much more difficult to put it into practice. Part of the problem is that even after baptism, we remain people *on the way* to perfect love—we are not yet perfected in love. So we struggle with the very real and necessary demands of daily life, and we wonder how it can be possible to add ministry in the world to an already-burdensome list of things to do.

There are no any easy answers to this question. Perhaps we should think of ministry in daily life not as something "added" to one's life but rather as its basic orientation. If we were to consider the issue from this perspective, we might see that our normal, everyday, sometimes boring, sometimes wondrous daily lives are packed with opportunities to make God's love tangible and visible.

The question then becomes one of seeing: How can God open our eyes to the need around us every day? It may begin with service you render in the church already—serving in the food pantry or visiting the sick. These actions are like the weekly worship in which we participate: They give a framework of meaning for what we do the rest of the week. Through them, though, God gradually and sometimes quite unexpectedly opens our eyes to see the whole world as God sees it.

Some questions that the newly-baptized should discuss in the formational group include:

- What does it mean for me to embody God's love and justice in ministry with the poor and marginalized?
- How do my spending habits serve God or fail to serve God?
- How do my patterns of consumption make more or fewer resources available for people in need?
- How will I make ministry with poor and marginalized people a regular part of my life, and so join others in witnessing to God's justice?
- What decisions do I need to make about keeping ministry in daily life an ongoing part of my life?
- How can I help the existing ministries of my congregation?
- How can the church support, encourage, and nurture ministry in daily life?

As with so many other dimensions of the life of faith, ministry in daily life is a practice with which we all struggle every day. Baptism marks the beginning, not the end, of that struggle. The good news is that we don't struggle alone.

This is precisely why the integration stage explores questions like, "What support will you need from other Christians in order to continue as Christ's faithful disciple? How has being in the formation group shaped your life? How is Christ calling you to participate in mutual support for faithful discipleship?" (*CTW*, p. 108) Catechists, sponsors, the pastor(s), and existing discipling groups in the church must make these questions a high priority. The process of Christian initiation is not complete without integrating people into ongoing settings for mutual support. Consider the following integration options:

- Covenant Discipleship groups
  (*For information, contact the General Board of Discipleship at [615] 340-7005.*)
- DISCIPLE Bible study groups
  (*For information, contact Infoserv at [800] 251-8140.*)
- Walk to Emmaus reunion groups
  (*For information, contact the Upper Room at [615] 340-7227.*)

The genius of John Wesley lay in forming people into classes for ongoing growth and accountability in discipleship; sustaining disciples is surely inherent in such formation.

RESOURCES

Banks, Robert J. *Faith Goes to Work: Reflections from the Marketplace.* Bethesda, Maryland: The Alban Institute, 1993.

Gurney, Robin. *The Face of Pain and Hope.* Geneva: WCC Publications, 1995.

Mar Gregorios, Paulos. *The Meaning and Nature of Diakonia.* Geneva: WCC Publications, 1988.

Sobrino, Jon, and Juan Hernández Pico. *Theology of Christian Solidarity.* Maryknoll, New York: Orbis, 1985.

Chapter Six

INITIATION OF CHILDREN AND RETURNING MEMBERS

"Let the little children come to me, and do not stop them;
for it is to such as these that the kingdom of God belongs.
Truly I tell you, whoever does not receive the kingdom of God
as a little child will never enter it."
(Luke 18:16b-17)

What is the goal of formation for children and returning members?

(1) To provide contexts for the formation of parents seeking baptism for their children and for the formation of youth baptized as infants;
(2) To form members returning to the baptismal covenant into people with a renewed relationship with God in the church.

The primary focus of the Christian Initiation series is the initiation of the *unbaptized adult* into the body of Christ. However, as *Come to the Waters* points out, many people are in circumstances significantly different from those of the unbaptized adult. Therefore, since "God's grace is not limited to one process [of initiation], the congregation and its leaders need to be skillful in adapting the process to those in other circumstances" (p. 67).

This chapter discusses two adaptations of the initiation process: for the initiation of infants and children and for the initiation of members returning to the baptismal covenant. The discussion focuses specifically on the role of catechists in the initiation of these two groups.

THE INITIATION OF CHILDREN

The first three stages in the initiation of infants or children (inquiry, formation, intensive preparation) focus on the parents and their responsibilities; the fourth stage—a stage that can sometimes take years—focuses on the youth preparing for confirmation. The catechist's responsibilities are different in each of these stages.

Parents seeking baptism for their children should have their own formational group; one of the church's catechists can deal solely with the parents.

However, if a congregation is small and cannot support a separate group, there are at least two options:

(1) Parents are integrated into the general formational group. Their experiences will add to the already rich mix of the group's reflection.

(2) The catechist and/or the pastor agree to meet with parents on an individual basis over a period of weeks or months. In either case, formation will happen.

Remember that the first three stages of initiation focus primarily on parents. During the baptismal service parents commit to provide the primary nurture and formation for their newly-baptized children ("Baptismal Covenant II," *UMH*, pp. 39-43). This commitment continues until the child discerns a readiness to undertake the journey of initiation, leading to the first affirmation of the baptismal covenant (often called "confirmation").

The catechist's ministry, along with that of the sponsors, helps to lay the foundation for the parents' ministry of formation in the home and in the church. With this principle in mind, let's consider each stage of the initiation process.

STAGE ONE: PARENTAL INQUIRY CONCERNING THE BAPTISM OF CHILDREN

As soon as parents request baptism for their child (during adoption, pregnancy, or after the child's birth), the catechists, the pastor, and the sponsors lead the parents in reflecting on what the request means for them.

In formational group sessions, catechists guide parents, sponsors, and godparents to think about the following themes:

• the experiences of pregnancy or of the adoption process
• the experiences of worship
• the experiences of living out the baptismal covenant in marriage, family, and child-bearing as a specific vocation and as an occasion for ministry in daily life

Respect the diversity of today's family situations. We cannot assume, for example, that every family will have two parents, and we should not talk about parenthood and family life in a way that belittles single-parent families.

In addition, any reflection on what living out the baptismal covenant means in the context of contemporary life has to consider the many challenges modern families face: violence, drugs, promiscuity, peer pressure, just to name a few. Honest discussion about these uncomfortable subjects can help parents raise their children in a life-giving way. The church can help provide spiritual support as well as other assistance: childcare, nourishment, and education.

Some parents may not have been baptized, or they may be members who have not retained a connection with the church. In the first case, urge parents to contemplate entering the initiation process leading to baptism; in the second case, urge parents to undergo initiation leading to affirmation of the baptismal covenant (*CTW*, pp. 138-150). This is important because the formation of baptized children in the home depends largely upon the participation of baptized parents who are active, fruitful disciples in their own right. It may be a heavy burden for parents to prepare both for their child's and for their own initiation. It may be appropriate for the catechist or the pastor to suggest that the first step should be the parents' initiation.

The stage of inquiry culminates in "A Service for Welcoming a Child as a Hearer" (*CTW*, pp. 130-133). The service is held when the parents have declared their readiness to sponsor their child for baptism. As catechist, it is your task to ensure that parents understand that they are entering a time of formation and conversion with a two-fold purpose: (1) to reaffirm the baptismal covenant for themselves; and (2) to seek God's guidance in shaping the life of faithful discipleship in their child.

STAGE TWO: PREPARATION OF THE PARENT(S) FOR THE BAPTISM OF THE CHILD

After the child has become a hearer, the parents enter a period of preparation for the baptism of their child. The next initiation service calls the child to baptism, through the parents (*CTW*, pp. 133-136); therefore, it is quite appropriate that parents begin to reflect on the questions the pastor will ask at the baptismal service. Also, during this second stage, parents may reflect on how living as faithful disciples will help their childrearing.

As parents, godparents, and sponsors reflect on Scripture, experience, prayer, ministry in daily life, and worship in formational group sessions, consider this possibility for formation:

- Begin extensive reflection on the questions parents will answer at the baptism of their child.

At baptism, the pastor asks the parents to renounce evil, to accept the freedom and power God gives to resist evil, injustice, and oppression, and to confess Jesus Christ as Savior, in union with the church (*UMH*, p. 40, section 4). They are then asked (*UMH*, p. 40, section 4):

Will you nurture *these children (persons)*
in Christ's holy church,
that by your teaching and example they may be guided
    to accept God's grace for themselves,
    to profess their faith openly,
    and to lead a Christian life?[11]

The first part of the question asks parents if they will raise their child in "Christ's holy church." Parents agree to nurture their child in the communion of the family of the *church*, not just their own family setting. Parents are committing their family to active membership in the body of Christ.

The question also mentions the "teaching and example" of the parents as a primary means of formation. The parents commit to provide both so that their child may one day profess the faith of the church.

Teaching means different things for different families. At the very least, it may mean that parents will demonstrate through conversation and practice how to be a Christian. They will teach their child to participate in worship and help him or her learn the Lord's Prayer, the Apostles' Creed, and the Ten Commandments.

Most important is the *example of Christian life* that the parents agree to provide. This is why the baptismal question so pointedly mentions the church in the process of parental nurture: Without the support and prayers of the community of faith, it is much more difficult for anyone to be sustained in a life that provides a positive example of Christian discipleship.

Help parents, godparents, and sponsors think about the connection between a life of faith and childrearing. *Come to the Waters* (p. 126) suggests the following questions:

- "What does your baptism mean to you? (Or if one or both parents are hearers, 'What are you seeking that you also want for your child?')"
- "How can you model ministry and prayer for growing children?"
- "How can you introduce your child to the story of salvation?"
- "What is the role of godparents in faith development?"
- "How can you encourage your child's participation in worship?"
- "How is life in the family an extension of worship and keeping time with Christ?"
- "How can you tell your child the meaning of Holy Communion?"

Obviously, these are not questions to be answered once and for all and then set aside. As the baptized children grow, parents will need to reconsider these questions.

STAGE THREE: PREPARATION FOR THE BAPTISM OF THE CHILD AND FOR THE RESPONSIBILITIES ACCEPTED AT BAPTISM

"A Service for Calling Children to Baptism, Through Their Parents" (*CTW*, pp. 133-136) on the first Sunday in Lent (or the first Sunday in Advent) ushers in the third stage of the initiation process for children. This stage takes up the weeks of Lent (or the weeks of Advent and Christmas) and culminates in the service of baptism at the Easter Vigil (or on Baptism of the Lord).

During the preparation time for the baptism of children, the catechist continues to assist parents and godparents in considering the responsibilities they will accept at the child's baptism.

Think about these possibilities for formation during this stage:

- Parents and their children will accompany the congregation through the season of Lent (or Advent). The worship and lectionary texts for both seasons contain powerful images that may help parents and children focus on Jesus. In formational group sessions, help parents and godparents reflect on these biblical texts. *Come to the Waters* (p. 127) suggests the following questions to help parents make connections with the lectionary texts:

  What is your vision, your hope, for your child as a follower of Jesus? What does it mean to release and trust your child to God? What is the calling (vocation) and claim of God upon your child in baptism? How like Hannah or like Mary and Joseph are you? How are you different from them?

- In addition to pondering the lectionary texts, continue reflection on the baptismal questions begun during stage two. It is unlikely that the group will have completed all of the questions during that stage.

STAGE FOUR: FORMATION OF THE CHILD IN FAITH AND DISCIPLESHIP

After children have been baptized, they are fully a part the body of Christ. Among other things, this means that they are to be included in Holy Communion.

At the same time, infants and children are obviously not prepared to claim the baptismal faith in a public, explicit way. Thus, they begin an extended, post-baptismal period of formation. The goal is to prepare the youth for the first affirmation of the baptismal covenant—often called "confirmation."

We need to rethink the length of formation. It is during this post-confirmation time that The United Methodist loses so many of its young members. Confirmation becomes a "graduation from church" instead of the beginning of a rich life of faith and discipleship.

Some writers have suggested that this loss happens because adolescence in North American society lasts much longer than it did even thirty years ago. We can no longer assume that all youth between the ages of twelve and eighteen are mentally, spiritually, and emotionally mature enough to accept something as weighty as the vows taken at the affirmation of the baptismal covenant. We expect saplings to be able to bear the weight of mature trees!

For these reasons, *Come to the Waters* does not suggest a specific age for youth to enter confirmation. Instead, it counsels parents, godparents, and congregational leaders to attend diligently to the spiritual growth of adolescents to discern when a youth is ready to affirm the baptismal covenant at confirmation. As a catechist, you are responsible for assisting the pastor in creating opportunities for youth to reflect on their journeys in discipleship and to help adolescents prepare for affirmation of faith (*CTW*, pp. 127-128).

When you and the pastor discern that an adolescent is ready to assume the spiritual disciplines of the faith as well as take responsibility for the vows of baptism, you should: (1) make sure that a sponsor is assigned; and (2) enroll the youth in a period of intensive preparation for profession of faith at confirmation.

As you work with the youth, consider these possibilities for formation:

• Do not offer a so-called "confirmation class." Instead, invite interested youth to formational group sessions for adult initiates. By doing so, you provide youth with an opportunity to encounter a mature exploration of issues of faith, and you allow an opportunity for people of different ages to interact.

It may be that through a combination of active ministry in the church and the opportunity to participate in formational groups, youth will be able to discern the way to faithful discipleship and to ownership of the baptismal faith.

In formational group sessions with adults, have youth ponder the following:

• "As a baptized Christian, how will you endeavor to follow Jesus Christ under the guidance of the Holy Spirit?"

• "What is your sense of calling? How will you offer yourself as a living sacrifice in the community of Christ's followers and in the world? How is God calling you to ministry in daily life?"

• "What support will you need from other Christians in order to continue as Christ's faithful disciple? How has being in the formation group shaped your life? How is Christ calling you to participate in mutual support for faithful discipleship?" (*CTW*, p. 128)

The period of preparation for profession of faith culminates in "A Service of Confirmation and Affirmation of Ministry in Daily Life" on the Day of Pentecost (or on Transfiguration Sunday). The appropriate service to use is "Baptismal Covenant I" (*UMH*, pp. 33-39). This is a joyous occasion, for those baptized as infants or children profess faith on their own and commit to a life of discipleship and service in Christ's body. Catechists should discuss with the pastor their role in the service; it would be quite appropriate for catechists to participate through the laying on of hands and offering acts of welcome and peace following the confirmands' reception into the congregation.

There seems to be a need in our churches for a rite of passage marking the arrival of adolescence. Many churches consider confirmation as such a rite. Instead, why not develop rites that commission youth for ministries in the church? Youth could serve as: public readers of Scripture, Communion stewards, ushers, assistants in Communion, psalmists, prayer leaders. This is not intended as a panacea; but perhaps by showing youth that the church values them and their ministry, the flow away from the church can be redirected.

THE INITIATION OF RETURNING MEMBERS

As noted at the beginning of the chapter, the focus of this book has been on the formation of unbaptized adults. Yet there are many people in North American society who have been baptized (often, but not always, as infants) but lack a relationship with the body of Christ. In other words, they are members of the church, but they have lost connection with a faith community. In addition, there are people who are active in their congregations but who experience a call to deepening faith and Christian practice. *Come to the Waters* calls the former "returning members" and the latter "searching members" (pp. 138-139). This section focuses primarily on the initiation of returning members; however, appropriate reference to searching members will be made.

Although returning and searching members have been baptized, it is appropriate that they enter a journey of formation that is similar to, yet also very different from, that of other initiates. The journey is similar because it also proceeds in the now-familiar stages: inquiry, formation, intensive preparation, and integration.

At the same time, the journey for returning and searching members is different because these people have already been baptized. The formational questions have to do with their desire to reconnect with the body of Christ; with their desire to respond fully to God's call for a new beginning in faith or to a deeper life of faith and ministry.

Catechists of large congregations with many resources may decide to create a separate formational group for returning and searching members. Where this is impossible, these members may join the others preparing for baptism in formational groups.

Why not re-baptize?

Before we talk about the catechist's ministry with returning and searching members, we need to address the question of re-baptism. Occasionally, catechists or pastors will receive a request to re-baptize. Often, the person requesting re-baptism has experienced a rebirth of faith and wants to express that faith publicly. She or he wishes to make a visible, explicit reaffirmation of faith.

For United Methodists, re-baptism is not an option. We believe that God's covenant in baptism is irrevocable. To re-baptize seems to suggest that God was not faithful to the covenant made during baptism. *By Water and the Spirit*, The United Methodist Church's official teaching on baptism, makes clear that re-baptism is not to be practiced (pp. 30-32). The *Book of Discipline—1996* (¶331.1.c) is equally explicit:

> The practice of re-baptism does not conform with God's action in baptism and is not consistent with Wesleyan tradition and the historic teaching of the church. Therefore, the pastor should counsel any person seeking re-baptism to participate in a rite of reaffirmation of baptismal vows. (From *The Book of Discipline of The United Methodist Church—1996*. Copyright © 1996 by The United Methodist Publishing House. Used by permission.)

Furthermore, the introduction to the baptismal services in the *Hymnal* acknowledges that human commitment to the baptismal vows often falters; but it also maintains that re-baptism would in effect indict the unwavering nature of God's promise in the sacrament (*UMH*, p. 32).

We need to keep in mind that requests for re-baptism arise out of a deeply-felt need for a visible and public sign of the working of God's grace in human lives. Such requests also frequently arise out of a misunderstanding of what baptism is. Requests for re-baptism will most often come to the pastor; however, on occasion, catechists may receive a request.

When this happens, the catechist needs to address both the inquirer's need for a public witness to God's work of grace and the inquirer's misunderstanding of baptism. Briefly talk through the experiences behind the request. Afterwards, the catechist may describe The United Methodist Church's teaching on baptism, inviting the person to explore formation leading to reaffirmation of the baptismal covenant.

Encourage the person to continue the conversation with your pastor; make sure, though, that your pastor knows about the inquirer and the request.

Sponsors and returning members

Sponsors play an integral role in the formation of returning members. Their role is slightly different from the one they play in the formation of other initiates. With returning members, the way sponsors integrate their faith in their daily lives will be invaluable to observe for returning members. They will be involved in helping returning members through the threshold questions of each stage of initiation; and they may be asked to share the practical wisdom gained in living a life of faithful discipleship.

STAGE ONE: INQUIRY

In this stage, the catechist's main task revolves around helping people discover why they desire to return to the church or desire to commit to a deeper faith. Formational group sessions could focus on the prayerful reading of the week's lectionary Scriptures with these questions in mind:

- What is the place of God in my life? What is the place of faith in my life?
- What is the meaning of baptism in my life? If it has no meaning, why not? If it has meaning, why?
- If I look at the course of my life through the lens of God's faithfulness revealed in my baptism, what do I see?
- Do I desire to enter a time of formation involving prayer, worship, ministry in the world, and reflection with other Christians returning to the baptismal covenant? (See *CTW*, p. 140.)

After the returning member, the pastor, the sponsor, and the catechist have prayerfully discerned that the member is ready to be welcomed into the congregation, "A Service for Welcoming a Returning Member" (*CTW*, pp. 144-146) will be held. This service may take place on any suitable Sunday. In the service, it would be quite appropriate for the catechist to briefly tell the story of the spiritual journey that has prompted the member to return to life with the congregation. The catechist (or sponsor) may also present the returning member with a Bible.

Searching members do not need to participate in the service of welcome because they are already active, "connected" members of the communion of the church. However, searching members also may desire a public beginning point to their time of formation. In this case, the congregation may use "A Celebration of New Beginnings in Faith" (*UMBOW*, pp. 588-590), with the adaptations noted in *Come to the Waters* (p. 146).

STAGE TWO: FORMATION IN FAITH AND MINISTRY

This period centers on the returning Christians' ongoing meditation about the meaning of Christian faith in their lives. This reflection happens in formational group meetings, in conversation with sponsors, and in the wider context of experiencing the church's life in worship, prayer, and ministry in daily life. The goal is to form in the hearts of the returning members a way of seeing Christian life that embraces the whole of human experience.

The formation stage shows returning members that being a Christian has important implications about how they live every part of their lives; faith and daily life must form an integrated whole. With this goal in mind, consider focusing on these questions in formational group sessions:

- Do I desire to profess faith in Christ and affirm my baptism? Do I desire to live with the church?
- What does following Christ have to say about the way I relate to my family members (spouse, children, parents)?
- What does being a member of the body of Christ have to say about how I make a living in the world? about how I (and my family) choose to spend leisure time?
- What does it mean to be a member of the body of Christ? What responsibilities do I have to the members of the household of faith?
- What does being a member of the body of Christ have to do with also being a member of the national and the international communities?

The formation stage ends with a service entitled "Calling the Baptized to Continuing Conversion" (*CTW*, pp. 146-147). The service takes place on Ash Wednesday, and it is integrated into the existing Ash Wednesday liturgy.

Why does this service take place on Ash Wednesday? Because the path trod by returning members is one of "penitence and restoration to the communion of the church" (*CTW*, p. 146), which in the historic practice of western churches has begun on Ash Wednesday and concluded with restoration to the communion of the church on Holy Thursday. The congregation, for its part, promises the returning member loving support, even while everyone remembers her or his unfaithfulness and need for continuing repentance and conversion.

STAGE THREE: IMMEDIATE PREPARATIONS FOR AFFIRMATION OF THE BAPTISMAL COVENANT

During this stage, returning members continue to consider their ongoing experience of conversion through participation in reflection on Scripture, prayer, worship, and ministry in daily life.

The chief question at this stage is: What does it mean to live in relationship with the Lord Jesus? Intensive preparation for the returning members' integration into the community of the church carries a specific goal: to enable returning members, at the service of the baptismal covenant, to renounce evil in all of its forms and to profess faith in Jesus Christ.

With this goal in mind, catechists may decide to spend time in the formational group sessions meditating on the words of "Renunciation of Sin and Profession of Faith" in the *Hymnal*. (See p. 34.)

There are three distinct parts to the renunciation of evil and sin and the profession of faith. Let's look at each in a little more detail.

(1) *Renunciation of evil.* Unlike the previous Methodist or Evangelical United Brethren baptismal services, "Baptismal Covenant I" (*UMH*, pp. 33-39) contains an explicit renunciation of evil. Returning members may initially balk at making this renunciation because it may evoke images of little red men with horns and pitchforks. However one chooses to symbolize it, evil exists. The baptismal service acknowledges (with non-specific language) that wickedness is in the world and that accepting the freedom offered by God in Christ means that one must renounce what is fundamentally opposed to God. As a catechist, you may find that the topic of sin and evil makes for an intense formational group session. Members will likely differ in their opinions about the definition of and the manifestation of the "spiritual forces of wickedness." Reflection should not dwell on the cartoonish aspects of our society's depiction of the devil or on the bizarre practices of the occult. Instead, help the group focus on the subtle ways in which evil discloses itself in today's world.

(2) *Acceptance of freedom and power.* Returning members renounce evil in favor of God as revealed in Christ. The second part of the renunciation of evil and the profession of faith, therefore, is an acceptance of the gift of freedom and power God gives in Christ to resist evil, injustice, and oppression. Ask group members to identify injustice and oppression in their daily lives and to identify how Christ gives them the power to resist. Invite them to think both in personal terms and in terms of the larger structures within which they live: the workplace, society, the economy.

(3) *Profession of faith.* This is the crowning moment of the service. Highlight that profession is not only an individual act but also a profession of solidarity with the entire church. In other words, the service of the baptismal covenant knows of no such thing as a Lone Ranger-type Christian! This may be easy to say, but how are we to put it into practice? A clue to the answer may be found when the profession speaks of putting one's "whole trust in Christ's grace." Ask group members: What does it mean in practical terms to put your whole trust in Christ's grace? What will you have to change in your life to make that happen? How does the community of the church fit in with this kind of trust? How do we encounter Christ's grace in the congregation?

"A Celebration of Reconciliation" (*CTW*, p. 142 and pp. 148-150) should be added to the liturgy on Holy Thursday. (See *UMBOW*, pp. 351-354.) In one sense, this celebration forms the endpoint of the returning member's journey of formation and penitence. Here the returning member is reconciled and restored to the community of faith. The entire congregation engages in acts of penitence and reconciliation, symbolized powerfully by a ritual of footwashing, imitating Christ who washed his disciples' feet. The whole congregation, including the newly-restored members, then celebrate Holy Communion together.

However, in another sense the returning member's journey lasts a bit longer, until the Easter Vigil when she or he reaffirms the baptismal covenant with the rest of the congregation (*CTW*, pp. 142, 150). Because this reaffirmation at the Vigil will have been the first in some time for the returning members, it is appropriate that returning members who are reconciled on Holy Thursday continue to meet with the formational group throughout Easter and the period of integration.

STAGE FOUR: CALL TO MISSION AND REFLECTION ON THE SACRAMENTS

During the Great Fifty Days following their affirmation of the baptismal covenant, returning members join the newly-baptized to reflect on how, through the sacraments of baptism and Holy Communion, God continues to call them to ministry and witness in daily life. With the newly-baptized, returning members explore their gifts for ministry. They also explore how the community of the church supports and nourishes their life in Christ.

As you minister to returning members, consider using the lectionary readings in formational group sessions to help them reflect on these questions:

- "As a baptized, communing Christian, how will you endeavor to follow Jesus Christ under the guidance of the Holy Spirit?"
- "What is your sense of calling? How will your life be offered as a living sacrifice in the community of Christ's royal priesthood and in the world? How is God calling you to ministry in daily life?"
- "What support will you need from other Christians in order to persevere as Christ's faithful disciple? How has being in the formation group shaped your life? How is Christ calling you to participate in mutual support for faithful discipleship?" (CTW, p. 143)

Work with the pastor and the initiation leadership team to ensure that Sunday worship during the Great Fifty Days stresses the interaction of the congregation with newly-restored members. With the pastor and sponsors, arrange opportunities for joyful celebration and meetings for conversation between congregation members and returning members.

The fourth stage concludes with "A Service for Affirmation of Ministry in Daily Life" (*CTW*, pp. 120-121) on the Day of Pentecost (or Transfiguration Sunday). With the newly-baptized, returning members may witness to their sense of ministry to which Christ is calling them.

RESOURCES

Refer to appropriate resources at the end of previous chapters.

APPENDIX ONE
FORMATIONAL GROUP SESSION OUTLINE

Gathering Time

Welcome and Opening Prayer

Reading of Lectionary Passage or Passages

Silence

Question

The catechist asks one of the threshold questions pertaining to the appropriate stage in the journey of initiation.

Silence

The initiates and catechist reflect on how the word of God in the lectionary reading or readings speaks to the question asked. The reading may be repeated, followed by another period of silence.

Discussion

The catechist leads a discussion of the initiates' insights and questions.

Break

Teaching and Discussion

The catechist or another person addresses a specific topic pertaining to Christian faith and practice, particularly as the topic relates to a specific stage of the initiation process.

Sharing Joys and Concerns

The catechist allows a brief moment for those present to share the joys and concerns in their lives that they wish included in the intercessory prayer to follow.

Intercessory Prayer

A sponsor or another person leads a litany of intercession.

Concluding Prayer over the Initiates

The catechist prays over the initiates, and then in silence lays a hand on each initiate.

Announcements

Refreshments

(For another way to structure formational group sessions, see the outline in *CTW*, pp. 154-155.)

APPENDIX TWO
A SERVICE FOR THE COMMISSIONING
OF A CATECHIST

This service may take place after the sermon, either during the congregation's main Sunday service or at a district-wide gathering of catechists. In this service, "presider" indicates either pastor, district superintendent, or bishop—depending on the setting. The presider and catechist(s) stand by the font or baptismal pool. If possible, the congregation stands and surrounds them.

The presider says to the catechist(s):

Hear what our Lord says to the church:
"I am the true vine, and my Father is the vinegrower…. Abide in me as I abide in you. Just as the branch cannot bear fruit by itself unless it abides in the vine, neither can you unless you abide in me. I am the vine, you are the branches. Those who abide in me and I in them bear much fruit, because apart from me you can do nothing" (John 15:1, 4-5).

The presider then addresses the congregation:

My sisters and brothers in Christ, *these persons* stand before you as *ones* called to the ministry of catechist. From the waters of *their* baptism, God has led *them* to this place; *they* have borne good fruit. God, the giver of all good things, has called *them* to labor in the fields of God's planting, to nurture, to encourage, to challenge, to teach, and to accompany people God calls to baptism and new life.

God alone calls and makes disciples, but God does not act alone. God has given the entire church the privilege of forming disciples as they make their way to the waters of baptism. Therefore, I ask you, the body of Christ and the garden of God's own planting: Will you do all in your power to participate in the ministry of formation embodied in *these persons*, so that God may be glorified through the lives of faithful disciples?

The congregation responds:

We praise God for *these persons* called to the ministry of catechist. With *them*, we will pray and work as faithful laborers in God's harvest. We pray that God's Word will bear fruit as people taste and see the Lord's goodness, and learn with us to love God and neighbor.

The presider asks the catechist(s):

On behalf of the whole church, I ask you:
Do you reaffirm the covenant made at your baptism?
I do.

Do you confess the faith into which you were baptized?

I do.

Do you renew your profession of the faith of the church?

I do.

Along with all the church, will you do all in your power to respond faithfully to God's call to make disciples, forming them in the ways of love, faith, hope, justice, and peace?

I will.

Will you be a person of prayer, faith, hope, and love, embodying the gospel to all you meet?

I will.

Will you be a person whose bread is God's Word and whose drink is God's wisdom?

I will.

Will you help all members of the body of Christ to use their gifts in the service of forming disciples?

I will.

Then, gesturing toward the water in the baptismal font, the presider says to each:

Name, remember your baptism and be thankful.

Here the catechist(s) may use or touch the water in a gesture of renewal.

The presider invites the congregation members to extend a hand in blessing over the catechist(s).

The Lord be with you.

And also with you.

Let us pray:

Loving God, we bless you for the many gifts you so generously shower upon the church. We bless your name for *these persons,* that *they* might serve you faithfully as *catechists* in your church. In your mercy, pour out your Spirit on *them* and on your whole church, that as one Body we may share in your work of renewing the world in the image of your Son, in whose name we ask this in the unity of your Spirit. **Amen.**

The service most fittingly continues with the Passing of the Peace and a celebration of the Eucharist, at which the catechist(s) may serve as minister(s) of the cup.

ENDNOTES

1. James Dunning, "Dynamics of Evangelization in the Catechumenate" from *The Catechumenal Process: Adult Initiation and Formation for Christian Life and Ministry* (© Church Pension Fund). Used by permission, pp. 113-114.

2. When dealing with teaching Scripture (and with Christian teaching generally), Christians need to be aware of the historic relationship between Judaism and Christianity. From at least the second century, Christian teaching has been tainted by anti-Judaism (the theological belief that the church has replaced Israel in the eyes of God and that God's covenant with Israel is no longer valid). In light of the many centuries of Christian persecution of Jews and the experience of the *Shoah* (the Holocaust), Christians are coming to see that anti-Judaism has no place in the church's teaching. The United Methodist Church has most recently addressed this issue in its 1996 statement, *Building New Bridges in Hope.* I urge all readers of *Echoing the Word* to read this essential document and explore its implications for how catechists form people in Christian faith.

3. To learn more about this, see Thomas Edward McComiskey, *Reading Scripture in Public* (Grand Rapids, MI: Baker Book House, 1991).

4. For a more detailed introduction to the practice of *lectio divina*, see Robin Maas and Gabriel O'Donnell, eds. *Spiritual Traditions for the Contemporary Church* (Nashville: Abingdon, 1990), pp. 45-53.

5. For a fuller discussion of the relationship between the Lenten readings and baptism, see Joseph P. Russell, *The New Prayer Book Guide to Christian Education* (Cambridge, MA: Cowley, 1996).

6. This third option is particularly relevant for congregations choosing to retain the Acts reading in place of the Old Testament reading during the Sundays of the Easter season.

7. See Ion Bria, *The Liturgy After the Liturgy: Mission and Witness from an Orthodox Perspective* (Geneva: WCC Publications, 1996).

8. The following two paragraphs largely derive from the discussion in Max Thurian's *Modern Man and Spiritual Life* (New York: Association Press, 1963), pp. 31-36.

9. Akron, OH: Order of Saint Luke Publications, 1995.

10. From *The United Methodist Hymnal,* Word and Table: Service I Copyright © 1972 Methodist Publishing House; © 1980, 1985, 1989 The United Methodist Publishing House. Used by permission.

11. From *The United Methodist Hymnal,* Baptismal Covenant II Copyright © 1976, 1985, 1987, 1989 by The United Methodist Publishing House. Used by permission.